Waterspouts of Glory

Waterspouts of *Glory*

Spiritual

Portions

for the

Spiritually

Hungry

Wade E. Taylor

First Edition
First Printing February, 1996
Second Printing April, 1997
Third Printing April, 1999

Note: Each passage of Scripture has been carefully compared with the King James Version. When different, apart from clarity, the King James version is used with "KJV" annotated.

PINECREST PUBLICATIONS
Salisbury Center, NY 13454

Contents

Preface

If you have fully submitted your life to the Lord Jesus Christ, are spiritually hungry and long for a quality relationship with Him, then this book is for you.

The primary intention of the pages that follow is to spiritually challenge each of us who recognize that there is **more** available to us than we have presently experienced. The spiritual food that is contained within this book is intended to not only satisfy our present spiritual hunger, but to set before us a map and a means of attainment that will guide us toward this "more."

> "Deep calleth unto deep. At the noise of Thy water-spouts, all thy waves and thy billows are gone over me" Psalm 42:7 KJV.

Our Lord is a seeking God who desires quality times of intimate fellowship with us. We were therefore created with the capacity to satisfy that need which is within our Creator. He searches *("DEEP calleth unto deep")* the hidden intent within our hearts for an indication of our willingness to respond to Him. If He finds within us even the slightest wish to truly, experientially know Him, He will demonstrate a singular interest in us.

This personal attention which we receive from the Lord to awaken such desire that lies dormant within us, can be compared to a waterspout which is formed by a wind pattern that whips rain into a funnel of water, then directs it toward a singular point of destination. While the rain showers upon all, a waterspout aims a deluge upon one, thus,

"All thy waves and thy billows are gone over me."

It is truly marvelous to experience this *DEEP calling unto deep* by which the Lord becomes singularly active within our lives and takes a personal interest in bringing us into a place of intimate communion and fellowship with Him.

At first we may not understand the purpose and direction of this Divine activity, thus the "*noise* of thy waterspouts;" but as we respond to His drawing love, this "noise" will gradually become within us "*a song of worship and adoration*" that will open the door which leads into His presence and purpose for our lives.

Our part is to respond to His call to us,

"Deep calleth to deep."

Introduction

An innumerable multitude knows Jesus as their personal "Savior." These openly acknowledge that He shed His blood upon Calvary's cross in atonement for their sin, and to some measure, live a committed Christian life. The name "Jesus" has become precious to them.

Within this number, many also know Jesus as the "Christ," or the "Anointed One." They have received the Baptism in the Holy Spirit, have experienced touches of His anointing, and to some degree, have been used in the operation of Holy Spirit gift ministries.

There are fewer however, who have received Jesus as their personal "Lord." To make Him Lord means that we have crucified our self-life, given up all right to our own lives, and have unconditionally submitted ourselves to the governmental rule of His Kingdom.

To know Him in this way is to personally experience Him in **the fullness of His Name**. He has indeed become to us "THE LORD JESUS CHRIST." Each aspect of His Name has become a personal reality within our spiritual life and experience.

Heaven is not the goal of our Christian experience. Rather, it is included in our redemption as our inheritance. We will be in His eternal presence at the end of our sojourn here.

> "For we know that, if the earthly house of our tabernacle be dissolved, we have a building from God, an house not made with hands, eternal, in the heavens" II Cor 5:1 Worrell.

Our being saved and filled with the Holy Spirit does not fulfill all that the Lord has provided for us. Even if we function in the five-fold ministry and in the operation of gift ministries, there is more. The redemption that was wrought upon Calvary's cross has adequately and freely provided all of the above for us. The Apostle Paul said,

> "Of this gospel I was made a minister, according to the gift of the grace of God given to me by the effectual working of His power" Eph 3:7.

There is yet more available to us. This "more" is something of great value, and is to be added to all that has been freely provided for us through His atonement. To attain to this requires an action on our part.

> "Then said Jesus to His disciples, **If** any one wishes to come after Me, let him utterly deny himself, and **take up his cross**, and follow Me" Matt 16:24 Worrell.

Salvation is essential for us to enter heaven ("*You must be born again*"). However, our submission to His Kingdom rule is conditional—"*If any one.*" This "if" indicates there is a choice which we are free to either make or avoid, without affecting our salvation. The quality of our spiritual life however, will be greatly affected by the way we respond to this conditional "if."

> "For the flesh lusteth against the Spirit, and the Spirit against the flesh: and these are contrary the one to the other: so that ye cannot do the things that ye would" Gal 5:17 KJV.

Since our ways are contrary to and "cross" His will for us, we must die to our own ways if we are to follow Him. We do this by dying to our "*self-life*" upon a cross which we form of our own choosing. We ourselves must take up this cross. As we do this and merge our lives into His life, we become **one** with Him.

If we choose to make Jesus our Lord, we must totally submit ourselves—body, soul, and spirit, unconditionally to Jesus, who totally gave Himself for us. We are to take all of the salvation "gift" benefits that have been freely provided for us through the atonement, **plus ourselves**, and give all this to Him. In dying to our own ways and choosing His way for us, we are taking up our cross and making Him "Lord" of our lives.

To experience "Salvation" means that I have repented, was cleansed by the Blood of Jesus, and have received Him as my Saviour. His righteousness has been imputed to me and now I am "judicially" perfect, as if I had never sinned.

To experience the "Kingdom" means that I have taken all that He has freely given to me, **plus the right to my** own life, and have given all this unconditionally to Him. He has become "Lord" of my life and I have yielded control over the totality of my being, all that I am and all that I ever will be, to Him. He is "my Lord Jesus Christ."

Now, that which I am "judicially" (His righteousness imputed to me) can become an "experiential reality" within my life and being because I have given the Lord the right and permission to cause me to become "*a full grown man, to the measure of the stature of the fullness of Christ*" Eph 4:13b.

Once I have done this, I will gradually realize that my spiritual growth and development far exceeds that which it would have been, had I tried to make my own way through life.

Thus, it can be said by those who have experienced salvation alone, "I have Jesus," while those who have fully submitted their lives to the cross and have committed themselves to His governmental rule can rightly say, "Jesus has me."

The requirement for entering His Kingdom is not beyond the ability of any one of us.

> "Blessed are the poor in spirit: for theirs is the Kingdom of Heaven" Matt 5:3.

Being "*poor in spirit*" means that I have set aside all of my own abilities and ways and have unconditionally submitted myself to His governmental rule over my life. Now, whatever He may do with my life will produce within and through me that which is of far greater value than anything I could ever attain apart from Him.

The "Lordship" of Christ in our lives does not just happen. We must choose to make it so, just as we have chosen Jesus as our Savior. The following steps are intended to serve as a guide in making this further commitment to Jesus as Lord of our lives.

1. Find a quiet place where you can be alone with the Lord for an extended period of time.

2. Wait upon Him until you become inwardly quiet before Him and enter His presence. While maintaining an attitude of worship, thank Him for who He is and for all His blessings.

3. Now you are ready to vocally, explicitly relinquish the "right" to your own life and unconditionally turn it over to Him. As you do this, you are giving to the Lord full permission and the total right to govern your life as He chooses.

4. In very direct spoken words, pronounce Jesus "THE LORD Jesus Christ" of your life

and ask Him for the outworking of all that this means, both within and through you.

From this moment forward, He is free to bring you into the fullness of all the potential that He had seen in you. You have now given Him the right to accomplish this. He indeed has become to you "The Lord Jesus Christ."

That this might become a personal reality within each of our lives, this book is intended to be,

A "prod" - to challenge us.

A "map" - to give us direction and purpose as a committed Christian.

A "goal" - that we might "*press toward the mark for the prize of the high calling of God in Christ Jesus.*"

It is my prayer and desire that you will be richly rewarded as you prayerfully read the principles and truths within each chapter of this book and apply them to your spiritual life and experience.

Chapter 1

Soul and Spirit

"And the Lord God formed man of the dust of the ground,
and breathed into his nostrils the breath of life;
and man became a living soul"
Gen 2:7.

When Adam was created he was formed from dust. Had he been formed of "clay" his creation would be more understandable, as dry dust cannot be molded. The natural man would like to believe that he had been formed of clay, as this would have made him complete and independent within himself.

However, for a very important reason, God **formed** man from dust, then **breathed** into him. This speaks of an impartation of Spirit which caused the cohesion of the dust from which he had been formed. Thus, man is not complete within himself. By Divine intention, Adam was uniquely made to remain dependent upon his Creator.

Man was created to live and function in two realms. Therefore, the Lord imparted into him the breath of "lives" *(in the original, this word is plural)*. On the earthly level, He was "formed." Dust—soul life. On the heavenly level, he was "breathed into." Breath—spirit life.

In the transgression, when Adam partook of the tree of the knowledge of good and evil, this "spirit-breath" level of life died, and only the "soul-earthly" realm remained.

> "But you shall not eat of the tree of knowledge of good and evil. For in the day that you eat of it, you shall surely die" Gen 2:17.

Apart from a redemptive act by his Creator, man is but dust. He is unable to "cleave" to anyone or to anything, nor is he able to enter into the purpose for which he had been created.

This is the reason why the natural man, who has not been redeemed nor given this impartation of Spirit through regeneration, acts as he does. He finds it impossible to cleave. There is something that must be "added" before he is able to function in the purpose for which he had been created. God must breathe Spirit into him.

> "And when He had said this, He **breathed** on them and said to them, **Receive** the Holy Spirit" John 20:22.

Now in redemption, that which Adam had lost was restored. This takes place through the "regeneration" of the Holy Spirit when we repent and receive Jesus as our personal Saviour.

When we experience salvation, we find within our being a new awareness of these two realms: the earthly (soul realm) and the heavenly (Spirit realm). The first relates to our natural life—"*And as we have borne the image of the earthly*" I Cor 15:49a. This is essential, for in order to live and communicate in our environment, we must be compatible with it.

We plant a seed in the soil and cover it. It grows; we pick its fruit, put some salt on it and enjoy it. We may not understand how brown soil produces red tomatoes, white onions, and green peppers; but we eat and receive nourishment from them because the earth (dust) of which we are a part, is the level of our natural makeup and function.

But there is more. Our "new creation" life does not end here, for the "breath of lives" had been breathed into man. This is the second aspect of our creation—*"we shall also bear the image of the heavenly"* I Cor 15:49b. We were created not only to live and function in the earthly, but also in the heavenly realm. But because we are spiritually dead due to Adam's transgression, we must first experience a "re-creation" of the spiritual aspect of our being in order to partake of the heavenly realm. Jesus told Nicodemus that he could not enter the Kingdom unless he was first "born again" John 3:7.

Man was created soul and spirit so he would be able to live and function in both the natural and the spiritual levels of life. The Lord had a purpose in mind, so He placed within man a capacity for his development and growth in each of these diverse realms. This is a marvelous thing: finite, earthly man having the capacity and ability to relate to, and commune with the infinite Spiritual God in the heavenly realm.

We relate to and communicate with our earthly environment through five physical senses *(taste, touch, sight, hearing, smell)*. Should we lose one of these, the others become more sensitive and we would still be able to communicate with our environment. Were we to lose two or more of our senses, it would become more difficult; but if all five senses were lost, there would be no means of communication whatsoever.

The natural senses that are operable in the earthly realm are functional in both the natural and the redeemed man. But there is a higher order of life that is available to the redeemed man alone. In our redemption makeup, we are given "spiritual senses." These are a counterpart of our five natural senses and are just as real as natural taste, touch, sight, hearing, or smell.

When our spirit is recreated through a new-birth experience, newborn spiritual senses begin to function within us. As these spiritual senses are cultivated and developed within us, we are able to sense His presence and hear His voice. We are equipped to function in the realm of the spiritual.

> "While we look not at the things that are seen, but **at the things that are not seen**; for the things that are seen are temporal, but the things that are unseen are eternal" II Cor 4:18 Worrell.

In our soul life, each of us differs both in personality and in potential. Many are born with natural gifts, such as a special ability in art or music. These natural gifts are given to be cultivated and employed.

A natural person can only relate to the earthly realm, but a spiritual person can relate to both the earthly and the heavenly realms. The spiritual person also has gifts or abilities in his new creation makeup. These are counterparts of natural giftings and abilities. These also are given to be cultivated and used.

> "Now concerning spiritual *gifts* brethren, I would not have you ignorant" I Cor 12:1.

The word "gifts" is in italics because it was added by the translators. This word should be dropped and the plural form transferred to the word "spiritual." Thus, we are to be aware of "spirituals"—the realm of the Spirit, rather than spiritual gifts.

> "And God said, Let Us make man in Our image, after Our likeness: and let them have dominion . . ." Gen 1:26.

In this verse we note three areas: the "image" of God, the "likeness" of God, and "dominion." The created potential within our being *(image)* must, through a time of probation, be tested. This results in the development of our spiritual capacity *(likeness)* and produces spiritual authority *(dominion)*.

Man had been created with this potential, or capacity, for every function of both the natural and spiritual life within him; but his spiritual life and function was lost in Adam's transgression. Only in redemption is this potential restored. Then, as we respond in obedience to the workings of the Holy Spirit within us and begin to cultivate a personal relationship with the Lord, a sensitivity to spiritual things is developed. This enables us to relate to the realm of spiritual reality.

The Word of God tells us that we have "*the mind of Christ*" (I Cor 2:16). However, we do not receive the benefits of this just because we are Christians. As we "wait upon the Lord," we partake of new creation life and develop a mature expression of the mind of Christ through both our natural and our spiritual senses. These spiritual senses are further developed and matured through our obedience to a process of testing that is designed to draw us up into a higher realm of spiritual awareness, understanding, and experience. The outworking of this takes place as we respond to His desire for a cooperative relationship with us.

> "Come, my beloved, let us go out into the field; let us stay in the villages. Let us rise up early to the vineyards; let us see if the vine flowers, whether the tender grape appears, and the pomegranates bud forth: there I will give you My loves" SS 7:11-12.

As the Lord tested Adam by placing the "Tree of Life" and the "Tree of the Knowledge of Good and Evil" in his environment, so also, we must face a process in which we are tested to determine the outworking of God's purpose for us. Therefore, these two "trees" in various forms are placed in our spiritual pathway.

> "And the LORD God commanded the man, saying, you may freely eat of every tree in the garden, but you shall not eat of the tree of knowledge of good and evil. For in the day that you eat of it you shall surely die" Gen 2:16-17.

The tree of life *(spirit)* represents our utter dependence upon and trust in, His provision for us. The tree of the knowledge of good and evil *(soul)* represents our desire to be independent to choose for ourselves what is right or wrong.

> "And when the woman saw that the tree was good for food, and that it was pleasing to the eyes, and a tree to be desired to make wise, she took of its fruit, and ate. She also gave to her husband with her, and he ate" Gen 3:6.

Although this appealed to every aspect of man's soul, the Lord had said "no," and established a penalty for disobedience.

Isaiah 53 gives a clear picture of the "Tree of Life" through a prophetic description of Jesus. The words within the parenthesis have been changed from "Him" to "it" so we may view the tree of life as being a type of Jesus.

> "For (*it*) shall grow up before Him as a tender plant, and as a root out of a dry ground: (*it*) hath no form nor comeliness; and when we shall see (*it*) there is no beauty that we should desire (*it*)" Isa 53:2 KJV.

Why did the Lord do this? It would seem to the natural mind that the Lord should have formed man from clay rather than dust, thereby giving him life and form within himself, and then make all things concerning him beautiful and desirable. But His ways are different than ours. He had a reason for these "trees" being as they are.

The tree of life was as a "root" out of a dry ground. The tree of Knowledge had beautiful, luscious fruit in attractive color. And a (?)friend(?) was there, saying, "Hath God said? Does He really want to take all this away from you? Does He intend to deprive you? Would God really do this to you?"

It appears that the Lord has made it easy for us to make the wrong choice at this point. This is because He is looking for a people who desire His Person, presence, and purpose, more than they desire their own self-centered soul satisfaction.

Therefore, we must make a choice concerning these opposite "pulls" upon our being. We can choose to satisfy our soulish, sensual desires, as expressed in the tree of the knowledge of good and evil; or we can choose the higher realm of spiritual desire, as expressed in the tree of life.

If we think more of our "soulish" desires, which are very appealing to our earthly realm of life, and choose to satisfy these rather than our "spiritual" desires, the development of our spiritual life and perception will suffer loss.

Because the Lord has such a high calling and purpose for man, there is a penalty if we make the wrong choice.

> "But you shall not eat of the tree of knowledge of good and evil. For in the day that you eat of it you shall surely die" Gen 2:17.

Adam failed and "died" as the Lord had said. This affected his ability to stand in the presence of God.

"And the Lord God called to Adam and said to him, Where are you? And he said, I heard Your voice in the garden, and I was afraid, because I am naked, and I hid myself" Gen 3:9-10.

This nakedness had nothing to do with Adam's clothing, but rather with the loss of the covering of "Shekinah" that had been upon him.

When Adam lost this covering of Shekinah, he was unable to approach the presence of God and hid from it. "Shekinah" speaks of His Glory upon man; it is the covering, or anointing that allows man to enter and then abide in His manifest presence.

As a result of his transgression, the Shekinah that had been upon Adam as a covering became external, apart from him. As a flaming sword before the tree of life, it became an "enemy" to keep him from the spiritual life that he would have gained by partaking of the tree of life.

Then the Lord took an animal, slew it, and covered Adam with its skin. This involved the shedding of blood as a type of redemption. Now, Adam was "covered" and brought back into the possibility of relationship.

"And for Adam and his wife the Lord God made coats of skins, and clothed them" Gen 3:21.

This covering was a substitute for the Shekinah that had been lost. It gave him acceptance, but man was still prevented from coming back into the realm of spiritual life that he had once known.

"And He drove out the man. And He placed cherubs at the east of the garden of Eden, and a flaming sword which turned every way, to guard the way to the tree of life" Gen 3:24.

Jesus died on Calvary's cross as the Lamb of God and became our covering for sin. But there is more in our redemption. On the Mount of Transfiguration, Jesus demonstrated that the Shekinah was to be embodied in Him; it was no longer to be separate from Him. While Jesus hung upon the Cross, the veil was rent and a way of entrance into the place of His abiding Shekinah glory was made for us.

> "Therefore, my brothers, having boldness to enter into the Holy of Holies by the blood of Jesus, by a new and living way, which He has consecrated for us through the veil, that is to say, His flesh" Heb 10:19-20.

The flaming sword is no longer a hindrance to our entering into this experience of knowing His manifest presence. On the day of Pentecost, it descended upon the one hundred and twenty as a friend.

> "And suddenly there came a sound from heaven as of a rushing mighty wind, and it filled all the house where they were sitting. And there appeared unto them cloven tongues like as of fire, and it sat upon each of them. And they were all filled with the Holy Ghost" Acts 2:2-4a KJV.

We can abide within the covering for sin that Jesus provided, knowing His forgiveness, but never come back to the place that Adam (we) lost of being clothed upon with His Glory and having his (our) spiritual senses quickened.

When the Lord came to walk with Adam "in the cool of the day," Adam hid from His presence. When He asked, "Adam, where are you?" Adam answered this question and talked with the Lord. Notice that we can commune with the Lord in the realm of our soul and never come back to the place of full and open spiritual fellowship with Him.

Many are satisfied with only the redemptive covering that has been provided for them through the atonement of Jesus on the cross, and feel comfortable to remain there. However, the Lord greatly desires His people to come beyond this position to a full redemption of all that had been lost. This includes not only the provision of a covering for our sin, but also the restoration of the original covering of Shekinah to make a way for His abiding, manifest presence in our lives.

Our spiritual senses only function as they are quickened, or sensitized in His presence. Their development must be cultivated and this takes time. When we experience a time of fellowship with our Lord in His manifest presence, or when we are quickened by a "moving" of the Holy Spirit and respond to it, our spiritual senses develop.

The Lord is looking for a people who desire a full restoration of all that was lost. We have experienced His forgiveness, but this must give way to the greater victory of a cooperative life with Him in the realm of the Spirit.

The Lord is restoring His glory to His people, and greatly desires to demonstrate this through the lives of an overcoming people who, having rejected the downward pull of their soul, have chosen the higher realm of spiritual life.

The Lord will have a people who walk with Him in the covering of the "Shekinah," His glory, and declare His manifest presence and power to a lost and dying world in this last day.

Chapter 2

The Personalized Word

"And the Word became flesh,
and tabernacled among us"
John 1:14a

The eternal, creative Word became the greatest revelation that God could ever give to man. His Son, the Lord Jesus Christ, was born of a virgin and dwelt among us in condescension as "Jesus of Nazareth."

As He walked the dusty roads of His day, the world saw a visible demonstration of the power and truth of the eternal Word.

> "That which was from the beginning, which we have heard, which we have seen with our eyes, which we have looked upon, and our hands have handled, concerning the Word of life . . . that which we have seen and heard we declare unto you, so that you also may have fellowship with us" I John 1:1, 3a

Each aspect of our life should be of such quality that the revelation and impartation of the "Word" which we hear and receive, will find both expression and fulfillment through us—the Word becoming (our) flesh, a personal reality in our life experience, to be seen and "handled" by those who surround us.

This will encompass our consecration to the Lord, our walk with Him, our fellowship with the body of believers of which we are a part, and our relationship to the world in which we live. In each of these areas, that which the Lord has accomplished within us should be evident to others as a witness to them that will convict and draw them toward the Lord. We are the only "Bible" that many will ever read.

In Acts 1:8 Jesus said, "*You shall BE witnesses.*" That is, we ourselves are this witness. Our growth toward spiritual maturity is nurtured and established through the application of spiritual laws and truths to our lives. Israel "saw" the deeds of God, but as Moses "walked" in the ways of God, these things became a part of Him. Through the life of Moses, Israel experienced the results of God's revelation to him; and only then could they begin to understand.

The "objective truth" that is set before us in the written Word of God, or in that which is written about the Word of God, must become a practical part of our lives through personal experience before it is really ours. The Word is to become "flesh" *(an experienced reality)* within our spiritual life experience, as the world both acts and reacts toward us. As we rightly respond to this according to the Word, only then will the world see His life manifested through us. And, they will again marvel and say, "*Never did any man speak as does this man*" John 7:46.

Once our lives are fully committed to the Lord, each decision or choice we make has a higher purpose behind it that transcends its present effect. It is very important for us to understand this so we might rightly view the results of these steps that we take toward true spirituality.

> "For we are His workmanship, created in Christ Jesus to good works, which **God** has before ordained that we should walk in them" Eph 2:10.

We remember most of our spiritual "consecrations" because they are made at special times, have a recognizable purpose, and directly affect our spirituality. We value these and hold them as being important spiritual landmarks.

Along with this, there are the multitudes of seemingly unrelated "choices" that we are forced to make each day of our lives, which do not appear to us as having any lasting purpose or value. We tolerate these, but think concerning them, "*If I could get past all these mundane things, then I would be able to seek that which has spiritual value and purpose.*"

However, the Lord views these seemingly mundane decisions quite differently than we do, as these are not merely arbitrary choices that must be made along the pathway of life. From His eternal perspective, varied circumstances are purposely placed in our path so as to provoke us to make decisions concerning them.

The result of these decisions will then become one of the "ingredients" in the composition of the "seed" (*that which we are becoming*) which is being formed by the Lord within our physical frame - our "new creation life." "*Behold the sower* (the Lord) *went out to sow*" (the circumstances that require of us a decision or choice) Matt 13:3b.

The Scripture tells us that we are predestined "*to be conformed to the image of His Son*" Rom 8:29b. The present development of this "image" can be pictured as "a seed" that is being gradually formulated during our span of life, which contains all of the ingredients that are necessary to bring into manifestation in the age to come, this "image" of His Son.

All that is needed for it to be fully revealed is the "soil" *(the atmosphere)* of eternity. Once we are there, our life in

Him, fully released from the husks of time, will come into full view and we will be measured according to the extent we have grown into the fullness of His image.

This can be compared to an apple seed. Every necessary ingredient to produce a tree that is fully grown and producing apples is contained within this seed. There is nothing that needs to be added to it. All that is required for it to develop into a fully matured tree is the right environment and time.

We often become confused when our spiritual consecrations or decisions, which seemed so outstanding at the time, fade away with no *(seemingly to us)* lasting consequence. This is because we only see the present effect that these produced. We do not realize that our consecration or decision became an "ingredient" in the preparation of the "seed" that we are becoming. Nor are we able to see the fully matured tree that will be released from this seed when it enters the environment of eternity.

When the new day dawns, the "atmosphere" will be present to release the pent-up life that we have become, which is contained within this seed. Only then will it be able to spring forth into its full expression of life. The life that will be manifested from this seed will be the cumulative result of all the ingredients (decisions), both good and bad, that went into its make-up.

Jesus said of this seed, that "*some fell into good ground, and brought forth fruit, some an hundred fold, some sixty fold, some thirty fold*" Matt 13:8. The quality of our consecrations and decisions throughout the span of our life determines which of these gradations will apply to our eternal estate.

The most important thing I can do today is to live in such a way that only the very best ingredients go into the make-up of this "seed" that I am becoming. Most of the spiritual consecrations that I make will not presently come to the full outworking of their intended purpose. There is not enough time within the span of our lifetime for this to happen.

However, these present spiritual consecrations and decisions are very important and have a vital part in the make-up of this seed that will manifest in eternity what we have become in relation to the image of the Lord Jesus Christ.

In eternity, the effect that these consecrations and decisions had exercised upon us will develop into their full fruition. There will be ample time then for the outworking of these experiences that present time was not able to accommodate. Much must be accomplished within each one of us in order to bring us to a compatibility with eternity, and into the cooperative relationship with the Lord that He both desires and intends.

The vision that was given to Ezekiel revealed a man with a four-sided face (Ezek 1:6-10). From one side, he appeared to be as a lion; from the second, a man; from the third, an ox; and from the fourth, an eagle. Each of these views revealed the same man, yet each demonstrated a different quality within his makeup. This vision was repeated to John in Rev 4:6-7 as four living creatures who picture the New Testament overcomer.

These four-sided heavenly views were the result of the outgrowth of a fully developed and matured seed. This understanding of the purpose of the Lord in forming a "seed" from the cumulative decisions, choices, and experiences of our present life experience is very important. It will both affect the quality of the decisions we make in our every day experiences and help us to rightly interpret life.

From the Lord's perspective, He will place within our pattern of life experience, all of the circumstances that are necessary so as to enable us to make the decisions that will produce this fully developed "seed" that He desires us to become.

A clearer understanding of these things will only be realized in the age to come, when the "seed" that we have become will be a life manifested as being like the tree of life, bearing all manner of fruit for the healing of the nations (Rev 22:2).

Then, we will understand the "why" of these present difficult experiences that we must daily endure, and we will be fully satisfied.

Chapter 3

The Word Becoming A Personal Reality

"And to the angel of the church in Sardis write:
He who has the seven Spirits of God
and the seven stars says these things.
I know your works, that you have a name
that you live, and are dead"
Rev 3:1.

This word to the church in Sardis also applies to those presently in the Body of Christ who are outwardly "letter perfect," but have not experienced that which they believe. They contend for the doctrines and precepts of the Word, yet they have not allowed these to change their lives. The Word of God has not become an inner reality, as they have no personal spiritual life.

For example, a minister who taught on the Baptism in the Holy Spirit presented the need for receiving the Baptism with intellectual accuracy and clarity. But he did not impart a confidence and desire that would lead others into this experience, since he had not experienced it himself. As a result, no one received the Baptism.

Later, another minister came and spoke on the Baptism in the Holy Spirit. His presentation was poor, but heavily anointed. Thus, he imparted a hunger and urgency to receive this experience because it was a personal reality that had changed his life. Needless to say, many received the Holy Spirit Baptism.

Dr. Charles Price was a gifted Bible teacher with an ability to present the Word with profound clarity and richness of expression. He once testified that he often sat at the feet of an elderly woman who could neither read nor write, but had received deep spiritual insight through spending hours in fellowship with the Lord, whom she had come to intimately know. Although she was unable to communicate these spiritual truths, Dr. Price was able to partake of them because he was wise enough to recognize the wealth of revelation that was within her, and humble enough to sit at her feet to receive.

> "The secret of the LORD is with those who fear Him; and He will show them His covenant" Psalm 25:14.

When the King James translation was written, the word "fear" meant a deep reverence and trust. Those who exhibited this quality understood that the truth they sought was hidden in a "veiled" form that was not available to the casual seeker. Thus, the Lord reveals His "secrets" to those who recognize and open their being to the "vessel" in which these truths are contained. This requires an implicit trust in the Lord that goes beyond reason, as the "container" may not (seemingly) be desirable.

Many years ago, a visiting minister spoke in the Bible School Chapel about the price attached to experiencing a personal knowledge of the Lord Himself. In conclusion, he invited those who were willing to pay this price to come forward. It seemed as if the anointing lifted, and no one responded. He repeated the challenge, but still there was no response. Suddenly, the presence of the Lord flooded the Chapel, and almost everyone stood and began to move forward. Then this word came, "you are too late." Their response was surface and emotional; the Lord was seeking an inner heart response. Though we missed, we learned a valuable lesson.

It is in the place where we feel the least spiritual that our commitment to the Lord really counts. In the richness and emotion of His presence, it is easy for us to make many promises to the Lord that will not be kept.

A story is told about a housewife who came to the altar after a stirring message on the love of God. She asked the Lord for a revelation of His Love. She waited for some time, but nothing happened and she went home disappointed.

When she arrived at home, she was greeted by her mother-in-law, who had unexpectedly moved in. The next morning, the maid was cleaning the house as usual, when the mother-in-law appeared on the scene. She promptly fired the maid and informed her daughter-in-law that she should clean her own house.

Before long, the housewife was in her bedroom crying, pleading with the Lord to remove her mother-in-law. The Lord reminded her that she had asked for an experience of His love. He told her to go and tell her mother-in-law that she loved her and was glad she was there. But she was unable to do so.

Later, during the evening meal, her mother-in-law said, "Is this the best food you can cook? My son deserves a better meal than this." Again, the wife resorted to her bedroom to plead with the Lord for the removal of her mother-in-law from her home. And again the Lord told her to tell her mother-in-law that she loved her and was glad she was there.

Finally, she gave in to the Lord, and with His help she was able to do what He asked, and to do it from her heart. Later, her mother-in-law appeared with her suitcase and said she was leaving. The love that this housewife had sought at an altar had been perfected within her in a real life situation. Now she had a personal understanding of the "love of God."

Often, we may be puzzled by the Lord's response to our requests because we little realize that He desires His Word to first become a personal reality within our being. We must be willing to allow this personalization of the Word of God within us through our daily life experiences.

At times, we find ourselves feeling justified in a given situation. We think we are entitled to the Lord's intervention in our behalf because we have done what was right. From a human perspective, this may be true. However, in the Kingdom we have no rights, as all is to be submitted to His higher ways and purpose.

In the year of Jubilee, those who had been sold into slavery were set free. But if a slave had a benevolent master and desired to remain in servitude, his ear was pierced with an awl that went through into the door casing as a witness of his willing submission. The dent in the casing was a testimony of this commitment.

During a chapel service in 1958, the Lord made clear to me that I still maintained the right to my life and I was given an opportunity to unconditionally submit it to Him. I went to the pulpit and confessed my condition and expressed my desire to give up my right to freedom and become His "love slave." Suddenly, the edge of the pulpit became as a door post. I bent over, placed my ear lobe on this "door post" and asked the Lord to "pierce" it, thus demonstrating giving up the right to my own life.

Some time later, in a situation in which I felt the Lord was not responding to my need as I thought He should,

I complained, "Lord, this is not fair." He responded, "You have no rights, you gave them up. Your ear has been pierced and I am free to use you as I desire." The Lord had something in mind that was of greater purpose and value than that which I sought.

I am gradually coming to know that His way is best and I can fully trust my life in His hands. He is a benevolent master who is truly interested in our well-being. We can trust His actions concerning our needs, even though at the time we may not understand.

Those in the church at Sardis were concerned about the "letter" of the Word (outward) and as a result, Jesus said they were "dead" (inward). The Lord is looking for a people who will allow the Word to become active within their life circumstances to transform them. These must submit their lives unconditionally to the Lord, and invite Him to come within to accomplish His purpose.

It is crucial that the letter of the Word becomes an experiential personal reality within our lives.

Chapter 4

Developing A Personal Prayer Life

Prayer should be a natural function of our everyday life and at the very heart of our relationship with our Lord. Therefore, our prayer-time should leave us feeling blessed and refreshed, rather than frustrated by struggling to endure the allotted time. If this is not true, we are not praying as we should.

If we are struggling, the allotted time we spend in prayer should be reduced until we become comfortable and leave refreshed. Then, gradually the time should be extended. Understanding the value of prayer will enhance our ability to abide in prolonged sessions of prayer.

Our need is not to be better informed about the principles and methods of prayer, but rather to be stirred to pray, thus experiencing the immeasurable value of prayer. The results and rewards gained by time spent in prayer can be known only by those who are greatly exercised therein.

Prayer should begin with a flow of pure worship to the Lord, which enables us to give expression to our love for Him. After this, we may express our thanksgiving for all He has done for us. We should present our needs only after we have confirmed that our lives are fully submitted to Him, and to His will and purpose for us.

However, it is not necessary that we have a need in order to pray. Primarily, our prayer life should be the expression of an on-going communion with our Lord and the confirming of our dependence upon Him for every aspect of our lives.

> "But rather seek the Kingdom of God, and all these things shall be added to you" Luke 12:31.

Prayer is the means whereby this dependent relationship finds its completion. It is through this union with Him in prayer that the Lord meets our needs. Thus, prayer is at the very heart of our Christian experience and growth. Out of an effective prayer life will develop a cooperative and productive relationship with Him.

If we are searching for some new revelation or fad to follow rather than seeking to find satisfaction and fulfillment through our prayer experience, we may easily be led into some form of deception. The foundation of our spiritual life and experience, of which our personal prayer life is a primary ingredient, must be established upon the Lord Himself and upon our submission to Him.

When Jesus called His disciples, He said: *"Come ye after me, and I will make you to become fishers of men"* Mark 1:17. Note that the emphasis is upon their "becoming" rather than on what they should do. Forgetting what the Lord really said, we tend to rush out and at once begin to fish.

There must be a time of preparation before any "fishing" can be effective. Fishing for men will follow as the normal outworking of a life of prayer and communion with the Lord. If we practiced what the Lord taught, many of the problems with which we cope in our Christian experience would cease.

The enemy greatly opposes anyone whom he finds earnestly praying. If possible, he would provoke these to stop praying and "do" something, rather than let them alone to spend quality time in prayer with the Lord. The devil knows the value of prayer and will seek to hinder it at all costs.

The saint who is determined to pray should seek to identify the source of these hindrances to prayer, and then rise above all opposition and distraction, and continue to pray with increased fervor.

At this critical hour in which we live, the Lord is calling His people to serious prayer. Throughout the Body of Christ at this time, the glitter and charisma of personalities and flamboyant ministries is fading. At the same time, the door to the prayer closet is opening wider than ever before for those who desire something more from the Lord, and who are willing to spend quality time in prayer.

> "But you, when you pray, enter into your room. And shutting your door, pray to your Father in secret, and your Father who sees in secret shall reward you openly" Matt 6:6.

It is here that the battle must be won. It is becoming increasingly evident that all else has failed to bring the Body of Christ to its desired maturity with the ability to exercise authority and power over the enemy.

> "The Lord GOD hath given me the tongue of the learned, that I should know how to speak a word in season to him that is weary: He wakeneth morning by morning, He wakeneth mine ear to hear as the learned" Isa 50:4 KJV.

> "And in the morning, rising up a great while before day, He went out, and departed into a solitary place, and there prayed" Mark 1:35 KJV.

Comparing these two passages of Scripture reveals to us that Jesus began each day in prayer alone with His Father. His disciples noticed this, and were stirred with the desire to pray.

> "And it happened as He was praying in a certain place, when He ceased, one of His disciples said to Him, Lord, teach us to pray . . ." Luke 11:1.

The answer He gave was very easy to understand, "*When you pray, say . . .*" In other words, Jesus said to them, "You do not need to be taught how to pray, but you will learn to pray by praying."

Prayer is far more than telling the Lord what we think He should do, and all the wonderful things that would happen if only He would do as we ask. Real prayer begins when we enter into such communion with Him that the Holy Spirit can pray the will of the Father through us.

This is a taking hold of the willingness of the Lord, not overcoming His reluctance. To our own hurt, He may reluctantly give us something which we continually press Him for. Consider the children of Israel who insisted on meat rather than being satisfied with the Manna He had provided. He gave them quail, but Scripture tells us that it brought "leanness" to their souls.

There are no shortcuts or push-button methods for entering into His presence. "Prayer" means spending quality time with the Lord.

When the Lord's people come to an understanding of the value of this place of prayer and communion with Him, they will be on their way to a life of fruitfulness in His purposes.

Chapter 5

Cultivating Our Spiritual Hunger

"Draw me, we will run after You.
The King has brought me into His chambers"
SS 1:4a.

This verse expresses in two words, a prayer that is vital to our spiritual well being. These words are easily remembered and may therefore be prayed often, "*Draw me.*"

Following the prayer is a commitment to the Lord that we will indeed respond to Him, as He creates within us a spiritual hunger, "*We will run after You.*"

Finally, the marvelous result of the outworking of our prayer and commitment follows, "*The King has brought me into His chambers.*"

This essential prayer, "*Draw me,*" relates to the spiritual hunger that in varying degrees is resident within each of us. This hunger drive, a powerful basic "urge" at the foundation of all life, seeks its satisfaction in many ways.

In the physical realm, a baby is born hungry. The mother cannot produce this hunger within her child, she can only nourish it. The spiritual hunger within each of us is a creative act of God that comes from Him alone. It cannot be produced or imparted by man; but only by the Lord.

The Lord will enlarge our spiritual capacity, as in faith we look to Him to cause us to become spiritually hungry. A primary means to accomplish this is to present ourselves before the Lord and actively "wait upon Him." As we wait, He works in our behalf and will respond to our desire for increased spiritual hunger and capacity.

Once we become spiritually hungry, we must be careful to separate this newly acquired spiritual capacity from other desires and not allow some substitute to *seemingly* satisfy it. Nor should we seek some other means than the Lord Himself to satisfy our spiritual hunger.

As we actively look to the Lord and prayerfully ask Him to "*draw us*," this hunger within us will intensify, causing us to cry out for its satisfaction. The Lord will respond and come to "sup" with us. As we welcome His presence and "feed Him" with our worship and commitment to "*run after Him*," He in turn will "feed us," fully satisfying our hunger with Himself.

> "For my flesh is food indeed, and my blood is drink indeed. He who partakes of my flesh and drinks my blood dwells in Me, and I in him. As the living Father has sent Me, and I live through the Father, so he who partakes of Me, even he shall live by Me" John 6:55-57.

Our Lord is a seeking God who is very desirous and anxious for our fellowship. He will, as we seek to better know Him, create within us the hunger that will lead us into His presence, that we might intimately, personally, sup with Him.

"Behold, I stand at the door, and knock. If anyone hears My voice and opens the door, I will come in to him, and will dine with him *(we feed Him)* and he with Me *(He feeds us)*" Rev 3:20.

This "knowing" has to do with our partaking of His very life, thereby becoming a part of Him.

> "For we are members of His body, of His flesh, and of His bones" Eph 5:30.

As our spiritual hunger increases, we will be motivated, or moved upon by the Holy Spirit, to wait before the "door" that will lead us into a relationship of intimate personal communion with our Lord. We do this by setting aside all that is earthly to seek communion with Him in His presence.

> "Blessed is the man who hears Me, watching daily at My gates, waiting at the posts of My doors. For whoever finds Me finds life, and shall obtain favor from the Lord" Prov 8:34-35.

We open this doorway into the realm of the Spirit as we respond to His beckoning knock. As we invite the Lord within and commune with Him, He will draw us into a deepening of our spiritual experience.

> "Deep calleth unto deep. At the noise of Thy waterspouts: all Thy waves and Thy billows are gone over me" Psa 42:7 KJV.

This increased sensitivity and responsiveness to His desire for our fellowship will induce Him to knock upon the door of our heart more often.

> "I sleep, but my heart is awake. It is the sound of my Beloved that knocks, saying, Open to Me, My sister, My love, My dove, My undefiled: for My head is filled with dew, My locks with the drops of the night" SS 5:2.

The Lord had been out in the night, searching for someone who longed to be with Him. This expression of a desire to be with Him, "*My heart is awake*" moved the Lord to respond.

You have a hidden garden, Lord,
Where You seek for Your own,
Bidding them come apart and rest
Sweetly with You alone.

Each flower reveals Your loveliness,
Each tree speaks of Your care;
Under the sheltering boughs I would sit,
Finding deep solace there.

Take me into Your garden, Lord,
See! I stand at the gate;
Open wide the golden portals,
Lest I enter too late.

Lead me gently upon Your arm
Into a place apart;
Take me into Your garden, Lord,
Receive me into your heart.

Thus, spiritual hunger is the foundation of our spirituality, and of our growth into spiritual maturity.

The next step is our commitment, "*We will run after You.*" The word "*we*" portrays every part of our being totally seeking after and responding to the Lord.

Paul said, "I am crucified with Christ: nevertheless I live; yet not I, but Christ liveth in me" Gal 2:20a. We may quote this verse and even testify about it, but there is a spiritual law involved. Truth is never ours until we have experienced it and it has become a part of us. Then we too can say, "I live, yet not I."

The Lord will respond to our commitment, "*we will run*," and will cause His Word to become an experiential reality within our life experience. He will accomplish this by arranging all of the necessary circumstances within our daily pattern of life to bring us into this personal, experiential understanding of the written Word.

Concerning Jesus, the Scriptures tell us that "*The* Word was made flesh, and dwelt among us" John 1:14a. Only as the Word of God becomes a personalized reality within our life experience *(flesh)* will we be able to witness to its truth with authority.

After being baptized by John, the Holy Spirit descended upon Jesus in the form of a dove. Then the heavens opened and the Father said, "*This is my beloved Son in whom I am well pleased*" Matt 3:17b. Although this was a tremendous blessing, there was something more that Jesus needed to experience before this word that He received from His Father could become "flesh" *(an experiential reality in His life experience).*

Jesus emerged from the water **full** of the Holy Spirit and received the approbation of His Father upon His life. Now, the "word" that had been spoken over Him would be personalized, or made "*flesh*" within His life experience.

> "And Jesus being **full** of the Holy Ghost returned from Jordan, and was led by the Spirit into the wilderness, Being forty days tempted of the devil" Luke 4:1-2a KJV.

This is even stronger in the Gospel of Mark, "*And immediately the Spirit drove Him into the wilderness*" Mark 1:12. Jesus was compelled by the Holy Spirit to go into the wilderness where He was tested for forty days; forty being the number of testing. By the end of this time He had overcome every temptation and had totally defeated Satan.

As a result of His overcoming obedience, Jesus was able to come forth from the wilderness in the **power** of the Spirit.

> "And Jesus returned in the **power** of the Spirit into Galilee: and there went out a fame of Him through all the region round about" Luke 4:14 KJV.

The "fullness" had produced "power" because truth had been personalized in His life through experience.

"*For we are His workmanship*" Eph 2:10a. The Lord is actively at work within our lives, not just to get us through to heaven, but rather to conform us to the image and likeness of Jesus Christ (Romans 8:29).

He still seeks those who are willing to submit to and endure this time of being tested and proven. An enlarged spiritual hunger will sovereignly be created within those who respond to this call into the wilderness. Here, these will receive the capacity and ability to come to Him to buy "*gold tried in the fire.*"

> "I counsel you to buy from Me gold tried in the fire, so that you may be rich; and white clothing, so that you may be clothed, and so that the shame of your nakedness does not appear. And anoint your eyes with eye salve, so that you may see" Rev 3:18.

The Lord is choosing out a people who are neither spiritually lazy nor content to rest in the comfort of the "fullness" of the Spirit that they received as a gift. These are pressing onward, even into the wilderness if necessary. They are willing to suffer intense hunger until they have been fed by the Lord Himself, knowing that afterwards, they will come forth victorious in the "power" of the Spirit. The world desperately needs such in our day.

Acts 1:8 states, "*But ye shall receive power* **after** . . ." Power in our Christian experience does not come as a result of our having received the fullness of the Spirit. There is something more that is required for His power to enter our lives.

After Jesus had received the fullness of the Spirit in the Jordan, He was led into the wilderness for a time of testing and proving. Here, through this process, the Word became power in His life. Now, when Jesus ministered, men became attentive and said, "*Never did any man speak as does this Man*" John 7:46. Why? Because the Word and the flesh *(His life experience)* had become one. This is the oneness which the Lord desires to work into our lives also.

Once we have received the Baptism in the Holy Spirit, the Lord will guide us into the wilderness experiences that are necessary to bring each of us into this experiential knowledge of His power. As we faithfully pass through these experiences, His Word and His presence within us will become more than just a testimony or blessing. There will be an impartation of spiritual power through us that will bring conviction and life to all who hear.

> "And they were astonished at His doctrine: for His word was with authority" Luke 4:32.

The Word tells us, *"For many are called, but few chosen"* Matt 22:14. Another way to say this is; *Many are called, but few are willing to pay the price in order to be chosen.* There is a price that must be paid in order to come into this place where His Word has become a personal reality in our life experience.

> "But ye shall receive power **after** that the Holy Ghost is come upon you: and ye shall **be** witnesses unto me" Acts 1:8a KJV.

There is a popular teaching, "The Baptism in the Holy Spirit is *power for service.*" This is true, but this

"Baptism" is much more than that. The "power" that we are to receive is the "dunamis" (*Greek for dynamo*) of God. It is the dynamic that first flows "through us" as a witness to the personalization of the Word within us, and then "through the Word" that we minister, as an impartation of "spirit and life" into the lives of those who will hear and receive.

When Moses went up into the Mount, the children of Israel said, *"All that the Lord has said we will do, and be obedient"* Exodus 24:7b. This was a tremendous statement, but they failed. The Old Testament is written as a testimony that flesh cannot fulfill the law of God. Of ourselves we cannot, but in the New Covenant the ability to obey is given.

> "And I will give you a new heart, and I will put a new spirit within you. And I will take away the stony heart out of your flesh, and I will give you a heart of flesh. And I will put My Spirit within you and CAUSE you to walk in My statutes, and you shall keep My judgments and do them" Ezekiel 36:26-27 (emphasis added).

The Baptism in the Holy Spirit is given as the fulfillment of the promise given in this passage of Scripture. It is the "power" of the Holy Spirit that will cause, or enable us to walk in His statutes. The "*power*" in Acts 1:8 is the same as the "*cause*" in Ezek 36:27. These are one and the same in intention.

Thus, the Baptism in the Holy Spirit is far more than "power for service." Christian service is something that we "do" for the Lord. However, this verse does not say anything about doing; rather, it tells us that we are to "be" a witness.

"Being" speaks of what I am rather than what I do. It is the expression of what I have become in Him. If I am "*doing*" witnessing, then I am telling someone about

the Lord. However, if I am "*being*" a witness, there is something far deeper. In "*being*" a witness, I am saying or doing exactly what Jesus would do or say if He were here. Therefore, I am a "sample" *(a living martyr)* of Him.

This Baptism will truly enable us to better serve Him, but it is more than this. Through His power being imparted into our lives, we "become" a witness that can be seen as well as heard. When Philip said, "*Lord, show us the Father,*" Jesus' reply was, "*He who has seen Me has seen the Father*" (John 14:8-9). Jesus was saying, "*My life is a witness of the Father to the extent that if you have seen Me, you have seen Him.*"

"*Ye shall receive power AFTER . . ..*" *The Baptism in the Holy Spirit is a gift. But, the power is only available to us* "after." We must pass through a time of testing in order to experience this power.

Often the Lord's people are led to make a consecration, and then are left hanging there until the next evangelist comes along and leads them to make yet another consecration. This pattern is repeated again and again with nothing further being offered. Our consecration should be the "doorway" that leads us into a new and further realm of spiritual life and experience.

We asked the Lord to "*draw us.*" Then we consecrated our lives to "*run after Him,*" but this is not the end. There is another step that we are to take, "*The King has brought me into His chambers.*"

Here, as I enter into and experience the intimacy of His manifest presence, I will receive His enabling power to guide me upward on the steps toward spiritual maturity in my involvement with Him and His eternal purposes. As I ascend, I will enjoy increasing degrees of communion and fellowship with the Lord.

> "He gives power to the weary; and to him with no vigor, He increases strength. Even the young shall faint and be weary, and the young men shall utterly fall. But those who wait on the Lord shall renew their strength; they shall mount up with wings as eagles; they shall run, and not be weary; and they shall walk, and not faint" Isa 40:29-31.

Herein is the secret. It is an assured fact that our strength will run out, but "*those who wait on the Lord shall renew their strength.*" When we enter His chambers and wait in His presence, the power of God flows into our being. It is extremely important that we spend time waiting in His presence to partake of His life. Only then will we have the strength to face the testings and problems of life.

Our Heavenly Bridegroom desires to bring us into His chambers to abide with Him. Here, as His Bride, we will experience joy unspeakable that is unknown to others. During these times of intimate communion, we are brought into a closer union with Him. In the closeness of this communion, we will receive of His life and strength and come into a greater understanding of spiritual principles and truths.

As we pray this short yet powerful prayer, "*Draw me*," we are opening the way that will lead us upward into the inexhaustible chambers of heaven. Here, as the hunger within us finds its full satisfaction, all that we had longed for will be found in Him.

"The King has brought me into His chambers."

Chapter 6

The Intent of Our Heart

"Who, being in the form of God, thought it not robbery to be equal with God, but made Himself of no reputation, and took upon Himself the form of a servant, and was made in the likeness of men. And being found in fashion as a man, He humbled Himself, and became obedient unto death, even the death of the cross"
Phil 2:6-8.

According to this Scripture, from eternity the Son of God had a position of equality with God. In order to fully satisfy the penalty for man's sin, however, He willingly set this equality aside to identify Himself with mankind.

Jesus experientially entered this position as our Saviour through obedience and suffering. He could have done so an easier way, for judicially this privilege was rightfully His because of who He was, "*The Lamb slain from the foundation of the world*" Rev 13:8. He submitted Himself to the disciplines and the testings of life that He might qualify to become our Saviour through His life experience.

> "Though being a Son, yet He learned obedience by the things which He suffered. And being made

> perfect, He became the Author of eternal salvation to all those who obey Him" Heb 5:8-9.

Jesus had settled this issue within His being, and His heart was right toward God. He was determined to pay the full price for the outworking of the will of God, though it would cost Him His life.

> "For the Lord God will help me; therefore shall I not be confounded: Therefore have I set my face like a flint, and I know that I shall not be ashamed" Isa 50:7 KJV.

Through His obedience to the will of His Father, Jesus humbled Himself and became the Lamb of God upon Calvary's cross. He died in our stead, and shed His blood that our sin might be forgiven. Because of His perfect submission and obedience, the Father brought Him forth in resurrection life and then exalted Him.

> "Therefore God has highly exalted Him, and has given Him a name which is above every name: That at the name of Jesus, every knee should bow" Phil 2:9-10a.

This name, "Jesus" (Matt 1:21), identifies Him forever with the redeemed for whom He gave His life.

A parallel to this experience can be drawn from the life of David.

> "And it came to pass, when they were come, that he looked on Eliab, and said, Surely the Lord's anointed is before Him. But the Lord said unto Samuel, look not on his countenance, or on the height of his stature; because I have refused him: For the Lord seeth not as man seeth; for man looketh on the outward appearance, but the Lord looketh on the heart" I Samuel 16:6-7 KJV.

Samuel would have chosen the one who outwardly appeared to meet every qualification. However, the

Lord revealed a different method of qualification—the intent of the heart. This principle is exemplified in God's rejection of Eliab, and in the selection of David for the throne of Israel.

Later, David was severely tried when Saul turned against him and sought to kill him; but under intense pressure David chose the Lord and His ways. His response to this time of testing is recorded in Psalm 27:1-4.

> "The Lord is my light and my salvation; whom shall I fear? . . . Though an army should camp against me, my heart shall not fear . . . One thing have I desired from the Lord, that I will seek after" Psalm 27:1-4a.

The Lord saw that David would choose Him in the difficulties that he would face, and later declared him to be "*a man after His own heart*" (I Sam 13:14).

Another example of this principle is revealed in the choosing of Jacob, a deceiver, over his brother, Esau.

> "Jacob have I loved, but Esau have I hated" Rom 9:13.

At first glance, this Scripture seems to indicate that "Divine approval" is either an arbitrary, or a sovereign choice that is made by God. However, the choices that the Lord makes are based upon Divine principle.

Outwardly, it would seem that Esau should have been chosen. He was the first born; and when his father requested meat, he willingly went out into the field to acquire it for him (Gen 27:1-4). On the surface, he obediently did the will of his father. However, when he suffered the pressure of extreme hunger, Esau despised the blessing of God and sold his birthright to Jacob for a bowl of stew, which offered only a present, temporal satisfaction (Gen. 25:29-33).

In a similar way, Jesus also said that His meat was to do the will of the Father (John 4:34). But when He faced this same test of hunger in the wilderness, Jesus refused to turn stones into bread in order to satisfy His hunger. Even under intense pressure, He put the will of His Father first and said, "*Man shall not live by bread alone, but by every word that proceeds out of the mouth of God*" Matt 4:4.

During the time that Esau was seeking meat for his father, Jacob was busy deceiving his father into imparting the blessing to him rather than to his brother. This seemingly should have disqualified him. But later, when Jacob was under intense pressure, the true quality of his character came forth.

Jacob fled from Esau and fourteen years later, was returning home with all of his possessions. In Genesis 32:6-8, Jacob was told that Esau was coming to meet him with four hundred men. Therefore, Jacob felt that everything he owned was in jeopardy. He humbled his heart before the Lord and asked for His help (Gen 32:9-12).

> "And he took them, and sent them over the stream, and sent over what he had. And Jacob was left alone. And a Man wrestled there with him until the breaking of the day" Gen 32:23-24.

Jacob sent all of his possessions toward Esau in two separate companies, and then remained alone to see what would happen when the first group came to Esau. His plan was that if Esau destroyed the first group, he would take the second, more important group and escape.

An angel, who was in fact the Lord, came and wrestled with, or detained Jacob during this time of extreme stress (Gen. 32:24-26). Jacob did not thrust off the angel in order to leave and protect his possessions, but instead he detained the angel until he received a blessing from the Lord.

> "And He (Jesus) said, Let me go, for the day breaks. And he (Jacob) said, I will not let You go except You bless me" Gen 32:26.

Because Jacob's heart was set toward the Lord, he put the Lord first, even when he was under intense pressure. Therefore, his deceptive nature was changed by the Lord.

> "And He said to him, What is your name? And he said, Jacob (*deceiver*). And He said, your name shall no longer be called Jacob, but Israel; for like a prince you have power with God and with men, and hath prevailed" Gen 32:27-28.

Jacob received a change of his nature, along with position and power. Esau, who chose rather to satisfy the present hunger of his stomach lost out.

God deals with us according to the "intent of our heart," that is, according to what we truly desire to be. The present state, or condition in which we find ourselves will be changed by the Lord if we truly put Him first and then trust Him.

> "For the Lord God helps me, therefore I am not disgraced; Therefore, I have set My face like flint, and I know that I shall not be ashamed" Isa 50:7 NAS.

Chapter 7

The Purpose of Submissive Dependence

"Who is this coming up from the wilderness,
leaning on her Beloved?"
SS 8:5a.

As the Bride emerges from the wilderness, there is a particular quality about her that attracts special attention. Something has taken place within her during her experience in the wilderness that has changed her. She has become submissive to her Lord. Now, recognizing her complete dependence upon Him, she is seen to be leaning upon her Beloved.

Our Lord intends each one of us who desires to be a part of this Bride to experience this change. We are to place ourselves in her "shoes" and walk with the Lord through the wilderness experiences that brought her to this place of oneness with Him.

Throughout Biblical history, the Lord often used a wilderness experience to test His servants in order to perfect His purposes within them. The wilderness speaks of a barren and desolate area. It is a place where our inner needs become intensified in their craving for satisfaction; but the means to meet them are unavailable.

> "And you shall remember all the way which the LORD your God led you these forty years in the wilderness in order to humble you, to prove you, to know what is in your heart, whether you would keep His commandments, or not. And He humbled you, and allowed you to hunger, and then He fed you with manna, which you did not know, neither did your fathers know" Deut 8:2-3a.

In the wilderness, needs can only be met through an external source by intervention. Thus, the wilderness becomes a *"set apart"* time in which there is an intensified seeking of the Lord, due to an utter dependence upon Him.

In contrast to this barren wilderness, the Lord had planted a garden in Eden which provided everything that could be desired. Its environment was one of both beauty and fulfillment, complete with provision beyond imagination.

> "And the Lord God planted a garden eastward in Eden. And there He put the man whom He had formed. And out of the ground the Lord God caused to grow every tree that is pleasant to the sight, and good for food. The tree of life also was in the midst of the garden, and the tree of knowledge of good and evil" Gen 2:8-9.

When Adam and Eve were placed in this garden, they were instructed by the Lord,

> "You may freely eat of every tree in the garden, but you shall not eat of the tree of knowledge of good and evil. For in the day that you eat of it you shall surely die" Gen 2:16b-17.

This requirement caused them to be dependent. There were two specific things to which they must submit; they were to eat of the tree of Life in order to maintain eternal life (*take . . . eat, and live* Gen 3:22), and they were to abstain from eating the fruit of the tree of the knowledge of good and evil (Gen 2:16-17). They had to believe the word of the Lord in order to remain saved, as we must believe His Word to become saved.

The only restraint to keep them from eating the fruit of the tree of the knowledge of good and evil was the "word" which the Lord had spoken. They were not to partake of its fruit. This tree was in the midst of the garden and was both desirable and available. Eve had observed that its fruit was good for food, pleasing to the eyes, and a tree to be desired (Gen 3:6). Herein was Eve's problem; the fruit of this tree was appealing. However, she knew that God had said "*no.*"

Therefore, when Satan approached Eve, he rebutted the word that the Lord had spoken by raising doubt; "Hath God said?" In effect, he was saying, *"Would God tell you to give up something that is really good, something that you like and want?"* Even though the Lord had said "*you shall not,*" the fruit was so enticing and seemingly so desirable, that Eve disobeyed and partook, and gave to her husband and he also ate.

Through this act of disobedience, Adam and Eve forfeited their position of "*willing dependence*" upon the Lord. They failed to "*overcome*" in the test that had been placed within the scope of their pattern of life, and were thus spiritually separated from God. As a result of this, the process of death entered their being and they lost all that would have progressively unfolded in their behalf as well. They no longer "*leaned*" upon Him (Gen 3:17-19).

The Word of God is silent concerning what might have taken place in their relationship to the Lord had they chosen to remain submissive and obedient to Him. The only clue we have as to what might have been is to consider the outcome in the testing of the "*last Adam,*" our Lord Jesus Christ.

Jesus took upon Himself, in human form, the identity of a new Adam, and then faced a test that was similar to the one which the first Adam had failed.

> "And so it is written, The first man Adam was made a living soul; the last Adam was a life-giving spirit" I Cor 15:45.

Jesus, as the last Adam (a new beginning), overcame in every situation where the first Adam had failed. Therefore, after paying the penalty for our sin on the cross, He was resurrected from the grave, and after a time of witness, ascended to sit with His Father in His throne. "*Even as I also overcame and have sat down with My Father in His throne*" Rev 3:21b.

An "overcomer" can be defined as one who submits to the Lord and then continuously abides in a leaning posture upon his Beloved. This "*leaning*" speaks of a complete trust in and dependence upon the Lord. It is the result of our having become submissive and obedient to the Lord's will. Being an "*overcomer*" means rising **above** all that is less than the Lord's known, or revealed best. It involves facing the test of the wilderness, and remaining dependent upon the Lord for provision.

In the testing of Adam and Eve, they were given the opportunity to become overcomers. Because of their attraction to "the tree of the knowledge of good and evil" and its perceived desirability, however, they chose for their own seeming good and failed to overcome. All spiritual gain must be tested, if it is to abide and become productive.

Although they were abiding in a perfect environment, Adam and Eve failed their test and entered death. Jesus, as the "*last Adam,*" had to face a similar test in order to qualify for the place in life that the first Adam had forfeited.

In contrast to the perfect environment of the Garden of Eden, Jesus faced Satan in the barren environment of a wilderness. *"And when He had fasted forty days and forty nights, He was afterwards hungry"* Matt 4:2. There was nothing available to satisfy the intense hunger that Jesus felt. It was then that Satan appeared to Him and suggested that He turn stones into bread in order to satisfy this gnawing hunger.

There was nothing inherently wrong with Jesus' turning these stones into bread, except that God had not told Him to do so. Jesus, refusing to act on a word from Satan, waited for supply from His Father. Had Jesus exercised His Deity in order to provide for His own need, He would have become independent. He qualified by remaining in that place of total dependence upon His Father for provision.

This was exactly where Adam and Eve failed, for Satan had said to them,

> "For God knows that in the day you eat of it, then your eyes shall be opened, and you shall be **as gods**, knowing good and evil" Gen 3:5.

Satan told Adam and Eve that they should act independently from God and do as they desired. They could decide for themselves what was right or wrong. Here, Satan was telling Jesus, just as he had told Eve, that He should act on His own to provide for Himself.

Jesus confirmed His complete dependence upon His Father when He said, "*Man shall not live by bread alone, but by every word that proceeds out of the mouth of God*" Matt 4:4. Because He had refused to act apart from a word to do so and waited, He was fed by an Angel at the direction of His Father. As a result, He came forth from the wilderness in the "*power of the Spirit.*"

> "And Jesus, full of the Holy Spirit, returned from Jordan and was led by the Spirit into the wilderness . . . And Jesus returned in the power of the Spirit into Galilee" Luke 4:1,14a.

As a result of His willing obedience by which He remained dependent upon His Father, Jesus is qualified to say to us, "*To him who overcomes I will grant to sit with Me in My throne,* ***even as I also overcame****, and have sat down with My Father in His throne*" Rev 3:21.

We will be tested as Jesus was, if we desire to come into this relationship of "*submissive dependence*" with Him in His Throne. Once we have chosen this position of "*leaning upon Him,*" we will then be led by the Holy Spirit into the wilderness *(a place of spiritual barrenness).* There, we will experience either a great hunger *(dissatisfaction)* or an intense desire *(frustration)* in some area of our being.

Then at a critical moment, when we feel that the Lord *seemingly* is no longer interested in our problem and that He is *wrongly* delaying His answer, the enemy will be allowed to come and tempt us. He will try to provoke us to act in some way to produce, or bring about, the satisfaction we desperately long for, which is presently apart from God's provision for us.

As we steadfastly refuse this temptation and persevere, in due time *(His time)* the Lord will feed *(satisfy)* us.

> "But He knows the way that I take: when He has tried me, I shall come forth as gold" Job 23:10.

If we will be patient during our times of being tested and wait for the Lord's provision for us, then we will truly find that "*Eye has not seen, nor ear heard, nor has it entered into the heart of man, the things which God has prepared for those who love Him*" I Cor 2:9.

The first Adam failed and lost his place, or position as an overcomer. This was regained by Jesus, who overcame as the "last Adam." He was faithful in maintaining His place of dependence and as a result, is seated with His Father in His throne.

Now, Jesus is offering to all those who overcome, a place with Him in His throne. These overcomers are as the one who was seen to be coming up from the wilderness, "*leaning on her Beloved.*"

There is no greater joy than that which comes from making a determined choice to become dependent upon Him, and then to faithfully abide in this new found place of "submissive dependence" until the greater day arrives.

Chapter 8

Pressing Toward the Mark

"Brethren, I count not myself to have apprehended:
but this one thing I do,
forgetting those things which are behind,
and reaching forth unto those things which are before,
I press toward the mark
for the prize of the high calling of God in Christ Jesus"
Phil 3:13-14 KJV.

In this personal testimony, Paul tells us that he is determinedly moving toward an attainable goal. To know this goal will make our spiritual journey through life much more productive. It begins with our understanding the purpose of our predestination.

> "For whom He foreknew, He also predestinated to be conformed to the image of His Son, for Him be the First-born among many brothers" Rom 8:29.

The Lord knew us before we came to know Him, "*whom He foreknew.*" We did not just happen; we were chosen *(predestinated)* by Him before the foundations of the world for a predetermined purpose, "*to be conformed to the image of His Son.*"

This speaks of an on-going process which requires of us our submission to, and our cooperation with, the workings of the Holy Spirit to accomplish within us this predetermined intention of bringing us to spiritual maturity.

When we accept Jesus as our Saviour and are cleansed of sin through His blood, through the regeneration of the Holy Spirit, we become a new creation, a spiritual baby.

> "Therefore if any man be in Christ, he is a new creature: old things are passed away; behold, all things are become new" II Cor 5:17 KJV.

Thus, we begin this process of spiritual growth as a spiritual baby.

> "Desire the sincere milk of the Word, as newborn babes, so that you may grow by it" I Peter 2:2.

Likewise, Jesus came into this world as a baby, and grew into the purpose for which He came.

> "And Jesus **kept increasing** in wisdom and stature" Luke 2:52a NAS.

While He hung on the cross, Jesus cried, "*It is finished.*" He had come to full maturity in being and in purpose. Now He had fully accomplished our redemption, thus making a way for us to become a member of His Body and grow into maturity, as He had.

Judicially, our redemption was fully accomplished upon the Cross and "*we are complete in Him*" Col 2:10. But experientially, Jesus, expecting us to grow into "the measure of His stature," became the fully developed head of an immature body, *a new-born babe.*

> "And this until we all come into the unity of the faith, and of the knowledge of the Son of God, to a full-grown man, to the measure of the stature of the fullness of Christ" Eph 4:13.

To manifest an adult head upon the body of a child would be unthinkable. Therefore, there is an objective that is far more important than our getting to heaven. The goal of our Christian experience is to "keep increasing" until we come to full spiritual maturity.

> "And we know that all things work together for good to those who love God, to those who are called according to His purpose" Rom 8:28.

The *"good"* that is referred to in this verse speaks of our being made conformable to the image of the Lord Jesus Christ. The word *"good"* comes from the same root as the word "*God.*" It implies that we have become, in some measure, like God. Because we are "*predestined*" to be conformed to His image, the Lord causes these "*all things*" to work together in order to bring about this higher purpose of producing "*the image of Jesus*" within us.

Salvation is a gift, but spiritual maturity is attained through a gradual process of spiritual growth. This process begins at the time of our spiritual birth and is comparable to the stages of our natural growth.

> "Until we all attain to unity in faith and to a perfect knowledge of the Son of God, namely, to a mature manhood and to a perfect measure of Christ's moral stature; so that we may not be babies any longer" Eph 4:13-14a Williams

If I were to tell a four-year-old, "you are a baby," this child would become quite indignant. No doubt he would inform me that he is not a baby, but rather "big." Children ever long to be instantly grown, but this requires a fixed, pre-determined period of time. However, our rate of spiritual growth is governed by a different law. This time can be shortened through our cooperation with the Lord as He "works together" all things in ways that will enhance our spiritual growth.

The first phase of this law requires of us a drastic reduction. We must set aside all ideas of our own spirituality and become as children, ready to learn.

> "Truly I say to you, unless you are converted and become as little children, you shall not enter into the kingdom of Heaven" Matt 18:3.

The Word clearly tells us that we begin our spiritual journey as a spiritual child. There are those who so emphasize the "realm" of spiritual maturity that being a child, spiritually speaking, is frowned upon. They reject, or set aside many areas of experience that *(they believe)* indicates spiritual immaturity. Any expression, or demonstration of "child-like" activity in being blessed, or emotional expressions of joy are frowned upon as a sign of spiritual immaturity.

Some mistakenly believe that the gifts of the Holy Spirit are no longer needed, and that they have gone beyond the "five-fold" ministry into a new "realm" as "mature" sons. They pronounce themselves to be an adult, instantly arriving *"to a full-grown man, to the measure of the stature of the fullness of Christ"* Eph 4:13.

Like the four-year-old, they claim to be what they are not. "*Therefore, leaving the principles of the doctrine of Christ, let us go on unto perfection*" Heb 6:1a. We cannot leave behind that which we do not possess. It is folly to regard ourselves as possessing more than that which has been fully formed within us. In the same way, if a child could be pronounced an adult and instantly become one, this "instant-adult" would be very frustrated and unstable.

Most certainly, our being spiritually mature is important, but we must begin as "a babe in Christ" and then progressively, fully experience each stage of spiritual growth. The experiences of one level of growth will qualify and lead us into the next. We need not hurry, nor should we fear being left behind.

As spiritual children, we should embrace and fully, unashamedly, experience all of the (educational) "*spiritual toys*" which the Holy Spirit places in our path. These "*seemingly*" immature areas of spiritual experience, such as emotional expression or demonstration, of which the so-called "spiritually mature" are intolerant, have a significant part in our becoming a mature, balanced adult.

> "When you are invited by anyone to a wedding, do not recline in the chief seat, lest a more honorable man than you may be invited by him; And he who invited you and him shall come and say to you, Give place to this man; and then you begin with shame to take the last place. But when you are invited, go and recline in the lowest place, so that when he who invited you comes, he may say to you, Friend, go up higher. Then glory shall be to you before those reclining with you. For whoever exalts himself shall be abased, and he who humbles himself shall be exalted" Luke 14:8-11.

To assume a position of "spiritual superiority" and proclaim that we are "beyond" basic spiritual principles and experiences is a very revealing sign of spiritual immaturity. A mature person is able to play with children and with their toys, enjoying both. The difference between them is that the truly mature person does this by choice, and then goes on to greater things. An adult can enjoy either milk or steak, but the child is limited to milk.

We do not first grow out of the "milk" stage *(blessings and gifts)* and then press into the "meat" of God *(experiential identification with Him through His dealings, testings, chastenings, and scourgings)*. There is a marvelous balance wherein the Lord works concurrently within us in each of these levels. Thus, in one area of experience, we are seen by the Lord as being a spiritual "babe" and are coddled accordingly, while at the same time in another area, we may be seen as an "adult" with much more expected of us.

As we progress though each of these different stages of spiritual growth, we are to fully experience all of the inner feelings, emotions, and relationships that apply to each particular area of our spiritual growth. This will enable us to become stable, balanced, mature adults.

If we are in reality, spiritually mature, we can afford to take a "lesser" seat in the coming "banquet" when the Lord will begin to move in manifest visitation and gladly identify ourselves with those who are in need. The substance of His life that we are progressively, experientially, growing into will benefit these and will become evident to others, opening further doors of opportunity.

Then, "*in the day of His power*," the Lord will be able to invite us to come up higher and be seated with Him, for He alone is to be seen as pre-eminent in all, and we in Him.

Chapter 9

Inviting the Lord Within

"My beloved is like a roe or a young hart:
behold, He standeth behind our wall,
He looketh forth at the windows,
shewing Himself through the lattice.
My beloved spake, and said unto me,
Rise up, my love, my fair one, and come away"
SS 2:9-10 KJV.

There are all too many Christians who are content with simply knowing the Lord as their Saviour, and in a casual way continue to be satisfied with the fact of their salvation. Also, there are those who have gone further and know the Lord as the One who answers prayer, heals, provides, gives the infilling of the Holy Spirit and imparts gift ministries; but they remain fulfilled with these.

However, there are among these many who are earnestly seeking "something more" from the Lord without understanding that for which they are searching. Many of these wonder, "what is happening to me?" This is because the Lord is causing them to become dissatisfied with all that had formerly satisfied them.

In the past, the Lord allowed these believers to remain content with feeling the manifestation of His power in relation to blessing, provision, and ministry. However, at this time, He greatly desires to take those who are being stirred with this feeling of "divine discontentment" beyond their present level of experience. He is causing them to realize that there is much more, to which they are being provoked to move into and possess.

The Lord is approaching these in a more direct way, to disclose Himself as a Person who has both feelings and purpose which He desires to share, and as One who seeks fellowship with us and our cooperation with Him in the outworking of these. He is looking through the "lattice" of our present experience, seeking to draw us to Himself.

He is calling us to "*rise up . . . and come away*" as He desires to bring us into a realm of identification with Him in which we become involved with Him in all that He is about to do in the earth during these last days. At the same time, He is encouraging us to maintain our on-going times of fellowship and communion with Him.

This is beautifully expressed in the Song of Solomon where the Bridegroom invites the one whom He loves to accompany Him in all that He is about to do.

> "Come, my beloved, let us go out into the field; Let us stay in the villages, let us rise up early to the vineyards; let us see if the vine flowers, whether the tender grape appears, and the pomegranates bud forth, there I will give you my loves" SS 7:11-12.

The outworking of this higher calling into a cooperative relationship with our Lord transcends anything that He could ever do for us. Here, He is seeking to make Himself known to us.

All too often we become satisfied with "the things of God" rather than going beyond these and coming to know "the God of the things." We become so taken up with our involvement in working for Him, or with the many concerns about our needs or the needs of others, that we fail to notice when He comes to us seeking a time of personal communion and involvement with us.

Our Lord is a seeking God who will draw us into a personal, intimate relationship with Himself, if we will respond to His seeking after us. The problem is that we become satisfied with resting in the fact of His omnipresence rather than taking time to seek His manifest presence.

Although the Lord has graciously allowed us to remain satisfied with our own ways in the past, the hour is so late and the need so urgent, that He is moving in intervention to bring about a correction. In order to accomplish this, He may intentionally withdraw Himself from us and stand in the shadows, outside of the *"room"* of our present spiritual experiences and activities.

He does this to call our attention to the fact that He is a person who longs to make Himself known to us. It is important for us to understand that the ***seeming*** withdrawal of the Lord's presence from us, and from all that we are attempting to do for Him, is a blessing that is meant to lead us upward into a higher realm of direct involvement with Him.

In order to bring about a change concerning our infatuation with the "things of God" and turn our attention to Himself, the Lord, trusting that we will notice Him, will begin to reveal Himself to us as One who is desirable and worthy of our attention and interest. He longs to personally make Himself known to us and spend time with us in fellowship and communion.

> "The voice of my beloved! behold, He comes leaping on the mountains, skipping on the hills" SS 2:8.

He is grieved when we do not recognize His seeking presence and fail to respond to His desire to make Himself known to us. This happens because we are impatient or unwilling to invest the necessary time in waiting upon Him, or because we are satisfied to remain within our past spiritual experiences, being content with all the blessings He has provided.

> "Behold, He standeth behind our wall, He looketh forth at the windows, shewing Himself through the lattice" SS 2:9b KJV.

The Lord will patiently continue to wait outside, until we realize that we need something more than all these things that He has so amply provided; and finally invite Him to come within our spiritual experience where He becomes the center of our interest, rather than all the things He has provided. It is during these times of visitation with Him that we come into an understanding of His ways.

> "Because you say, I am rich and increased with goods and have need of nothing . . . I stand at the door and knock. If anyone hears My voice and opens the door, I will come in to him, and will dine with him, and he with Me" Rev 3:17a,20.

The above passage of Scripture expresses the Lord's desire for our fellowship. He does not intend for us to remain in our present state of spiritual barrenness, but longs to bring us into the experiential reality of personally knowing Him and His abiding presence.

> "He who has My commandments and keeps them, he it is who loves Me. And he who loves Me shall be loved by My Father, and I will love him, and will reveal Myself to him" John 14:21.

The experience of "*His manifest presence*" is conditional upon our keeping His commandments. As we die to our self-will and respond to Him in obedience, He will be released to manifest, or to make Himself intimately known to us.

His omni-presence refers to the feeling of His presence as power, or as a quickening of feelings, apart from His person. His manifest presence refers to the revelation of Him as a person with feelings and desires.

The word "manifest" means that He causes us to become aware of His openly revealed presence through one or more of our five natural senses. He does this, not figuratively, or in types and shadows, but as a present spiritual reality. His manifest presence begins at the point where we transcend the "letter" of the Word and enter into the "spirit" of the Word.

As we experience His manifest presence, He will reveal Himself to us in one or more ways by inviting us to enter into a cooperative relationship with Him. For example, He may lead us to quietly wait upon Him in His revealed presence. Or, He may move upon us in a powerful way that creates within us a greater capacity for His presence, into which He can enter and thus make Himself or His purpose known.

He may quicken us to a special understanding of His Word by bringing us into an experiential identification with the experiences of those within the recorded Word. Or, perhaps He will reveal something He desires to accomplish, and show us our responsibility and part in its outworking, and then guide us through the outworking of it to its full completion and satisfaction.

He may share with those who have experienced in some measure *"the fellowship of His sufferings,"* a specific burden for intercession or prayer and then guide them through the full process of "birthing" the answer to this need.

The possibilities are innumerable and marvelous. Because the Lord seeks to reveal Himself to us as a person who has feelings and desires which He longs to share, He cannot remain satisfied with a relationship that is only based upon our needs being met and our being blessed. Our feeling His quickened presence within, apart from His person, is a marvelous and desirable blessing, but it falls far short of His intention for us.

The Lord has been hurt so many times by those who take His presence lightly that He is both reluctant and slow to openly reveal Himself. Therefore, He will approach us very cautiously to see if we are really interested in Him, for Himself. In this instance, those who are intently searching for "something more" will quickly notice whenever He may withdraw His presence from them, and will urgently ask Him to return. The Lord will respond to this invitation. Then He will express to these a word of direction and purpose.

> "My Beloved spoke, and said to me, Rise up, My love, my beautiful one, and come away" SS 2:10.

The Lord has something far better to offer us if we will respond to His call to "*rise up*" with Him into a higher realm of spiritual reality. To this urgent call, He adds a word of encouragement,

> "For lo, the winter is past, the rain is over and gone; the flowers appear on the earth; the time of the singing of birds is come, and the voice of the turtle is heard in our land" SS 2:11-12 KJV.

We are living in the time of the "birth pains" of the coming Millennial Kingdom. Herein is the cause of our wondering, "*What is happening?*" as we feel within us these birthing pains that lead upward toward this new day.

Rise up on the wings of the Dove,
At the call of love,
Rise up,
To the courts above.

Rise up, earth's chains are broken,
The heavens open,
Rise up,
The Lord has spoken.

Blessed is the one whom He has called
To His high and holy dwelling.
Blessed is he who thus is stirred,
By the voice of Love impelled.

Winter has departed now at last,
Flowers are appearing on the earth;
And all creation is awaiting,
A restoration and new birth.

The *winter* represents a time of barrenness in our spiritual experience. It is a period of time during which the Lord is seemingly absent from us, and in which there is little or no quickening of the Holy Spirit within us or in our ministry.

The rain being *over and gone* means that we have not always been in the condition of a spiritual Winter. The charismatic visitation was given as a time of refreshing to prepare us for a further visitation of the Lord. But as wonderful as it was in its day, it accomplished its purpose and has come to an end.

The winter season being *past* speaks of a present opportunity for individuals to be birthed into a new realm of spiritual life and experience.

The flowers appearing reveals a present surge of spiritual growth within those who were affected by the past visitation with the resultant *fruit of the spirit* becoming beautiful to the observer. Our repentant response to His withdrawal has therefore produced within us a spiritual breakthrough. Now the initiative has passed to Him. We are abiding in Him, and He in us. Our lives and ministry are producing results that were never before realized.

The quickened, anointed worship that flows up to the Lord from deep within us is represented by *the singing of birds*. The *voice of the turtle* is a prophetic voice, speaking forth His word with substance and power.

These experiences that result from His indwelling life do not come through any intellectual comprehension or understanding of His Word alone. They require the impartation of His life to us as we fellowship *(sup)* with Him. Only then can there be any impartation of *spirit and life* from us to others.

> "Behold, I stand at the door and knock. If anyone hears My voice and opens the door, I will come in to him, and will dine with him, and he with Me" Rev 3:20.

The Lord is presently waiting without, looking through the "window" of the room of our present spiritual experience. We must quickly respond to His call to *rise up . . . and come away*. It is essential that we invite the Lord to come within and give Him full control over our spiritual experience and lives.

If we do so, then nothing that we could obtain while remaining in a lesser realm, could compare with this.

Chapter 10

The Secret Place

"Deep calleth unto deep. At the noise of thy waterspouts,
all thy waves and thy billows are gone over me"
Psalm 42:7 KJV.

The Psalms of David are filled with the heart-cry of a man who sought a deep personal relationship with the Lord Himself. Again and again, David expressed a burning desire to intimately know the Lord on two different levels of experience.

First, he longed to know the Lord face to face.

> "As the hart pants after the water brooks, so my soul pants after You, O God. My soul thirsts for God, for the living God; when shall I come and appear before God?" Psalm 42:1-2.

Here, the psalmist is seeking a personal relationship with the Lord in which he would be able to share his heart feelings and desires, knowing that the Lord would hear and understand the cry of His heart. David had a very special relationship to the Lord (Acts 13:22).

Second, he desired to know the Lord as one in whom he could place infinite trust.

> "In God I have put my trust. I will not be afraid what man can do to me" Psalm 56:11.

> "The Lord is my light and my salvation; whom shall I fear? The Lord is the strength of my life, of whom shall I be afraid?" Psalm 27:1

The psalmist had come into a relationship with the Lord in which he had many experiences in receiving the portion of wisdom, provision, or protection that was needed during a time of need. As a result, there was created within him a deep trust in the Lord.

When David failed the Lord, he deeply repented.

> "I confessed my sin to You, and my iniquity I have not hidden. I said, I will confess my transgression to the Lord, and You forgave the iniquity of my sin" Psalm 32:5.

Being set free from all guilt and condemnation, David could now sing the song that burst forth from deep within him,

> "You are my hiding place; You shall preserve me from trouble; You shall circle me with songs of deliverance" Psalm 32:7.

In response to this new level of relationship and trust, the Lord gave a very encouraging promise of guidance to David that he might never again fall into sin—if he would harken to this word and return to the intimate place of fellowship that he once knew.

> "I will instruct you and teach you in the way you should go; I will guide you with My eye" Psalm 32:8 NKJ.

David's repentance had brought him into such a close intimate relationship with the Lord *("I will guide you with my eye")*, that he could actually "feel" the intention of the Lord concerning him.

In order to maintain this new found experience of His abiding presence and intimate guidance, the Lord exhorted David to be perceptive and obedient to both His directive and corrective guidance.

> "Be not like the horse, or like the mule, who have no understanding, whose mouth must be held in with bit and bridle, so they do not come near you" Psalm 32:9.

Each one of us should experience this clarity of Holy Spirit led guidance, which is all too neglected, or absent from among the Lord's people today. As world pressures and dangers escalate, it is becoming increasingly important that we heed this exhortation to quickly respond to His directive guidance through the leadings and promptings of the Holy Spirit.

In Psalm 91:1-10, the Lord promises deliverance and victory in the time of trouble to "*He who dwells in the secret place of the Most High.*" We must clearly hear this promise with our spiritual ears, then appropriate these words into our being and digest them until they become personalized and real within us.

The Lord seeks a people who will choose Him for Himself alone, apart from what He is able to do for them in blessing and provision. There are many distracting influences that can, and if possible will, draw us away from a true, sincere devotion to the Lord. These forces endeavor to control us, but are only able to do so through our own choosing or allowing. It is very important that we clearly understand that the Lord will not over-ride our will. He does however, have ways to make us willing. He calls, draws, and guides us, but we are allowed the freedom to choose in every area of our life. Thus, we must choose to respond to His wooing of our hearts into this place of the "*secret abode of intimacy with Him.*"

The "pulls" away from this secret place are many. Always before us looms the subtle desire to be recognized or to be successful; to find earthly security by making provision against what might happen. All of these things will obscure Jesus and our dependence upon Him, if we allow them to do so.

We easily forget His promise in John 16:33b, "*In the world you shall have tribulation, but be of good cheer, I have overcome the world.*" Here, Jesus is saying, "*Do not fear, in me you may have peace.*" He has promised to care for us, for He is the Shepherd and we are His flock. In Him, we partake of all that He has won in our behalf, as we have need.

If we are not receiving His care and protection, it is because we have either chosen the wrong dwelling place, or we have set our affection on something other than Him. When this happens, He patiently waits, ready and willing to help us when we turn to Him. His Word instructs us to find and enter "*the secret place*" where He dwells, and then to make this our abiding place. This means that we have given up and committed to the cross our desires and ways, and have unconditionally submitted ourselves to abide in His pathway for us.

A wonderful joy is flooding my heart
Since Jesus has shown His love to me;
Into His garden He drew me apart,
And now His grace and beauty I see.

Jesus loves me truly, this I know,
For my soul, His life He gave a sacrifice;
Sorrow is gone and my joy complete,
His love has made my heart a Paradise.

Let me sit in His garden
and bask in His sunlight,
For in my heart He reigns,
As King upon His throne.

David erected a tent on Mount Zion for God to dwell in, but David's heart became the Lord's abode as he fully opened his being for the King of kings to enter within. The Lord said that He will reward those who seek Him. This reward is God Himself; nothing can compare to this eternal treasure.

In Romans chapter 8, we are presented with exhortations, promises, and the marvelous word that *"all things work together for good to those who love God."*

This may be read, "*God works all things together for good to them who make Him their secret abode.*" Then comes the encouraging word, "*If God is for us, who can be against us*?" Rom 8:31b.

We must put our trust completely in the Lord and seek our place of abiding rest in His manifest presence. As we do this, we will become eternally satisfied.

Chapter 11

The Power Of Choice

"And He said to all, If anyone desires to come after Me, let him deny himself and take up his cross daily and follow Me" Luke 9:23.

Each one of us who desires to fully know and serve our Lord will be challenged to make this life-changing decision to take up **our** cross. This is an option *(if)* that is not essential to our salvation, but will greatly affect our present walk and our eternal position in the ages to come.

As we prayerfully respond to this challenge, the taking up of our cross will become a practical daily reality in our lives as we partake in the outworking of our identification with the life and ministry of the Lord. As a result, a deep sense of satisfaction and fulfillment will settle into our being.

Many do not realize or take seriously, the tremendous value of what our Lord is offering us. Our part is to respond to His voice and follow Him in complete submission to His will and purpose.

"Come, my beloved, let us go out into the field, let us stay in the villages. Let us rise up early to the vineyards; let us see if the vine flowers, whether the tender grape appears, and the pomegranates bud forth: there will I give you My loves" SS 7:11-12.

The Word of God tells us that we cannot earn or merit our salvation in any way.

> "For by grace you are saved through faith, and that not of yourselves; it is the gift of God, not of works, lest anyone should boast" Eph 2:8-9

Once we have received this gift of eternal life however, we begin to face choices that will affect the rate of our spiritual growth, and our position within His body presently, and in the ages that are before us. Therefore, it is of eternal importance that we come to understand that there are spiritual laws which apply to our spiritual development.

> "**If** you are willing and obedient, you shall eat the good of the land" Isa 1:19.

The "If" indicates there are "conditions" that must be met before we will be enabled to partake of the spiritual nourishment which is promised. We must rightly respond to these conditional promises in order to receive the benefits that are offered.

To be "*willing and obedient*" is to be one with our Lord in both thought and action. This means our will is relinquished and merged into His will. The "*good of the land*," of which we are to partake, results from this oneness with Him.

Our unconditional submission to the Lord releases Him to invite us to partake with Him in that which He is about to do, "*Come my beloved . . . let us rise up early to the vineyards.*" As we walk in union with Him, we will receive spiritual strength and understanding which will enable us to expand spiritually and fully follow Him.

The Lord is much more interested in our coming into a "quality" relationship with Him than we are. Yet He is a perfect gentleman and will not force either Himself or His desire for us, upon us. Thus, He begins each of these promises with a conditional "*If.*" We must make the choice.

The Lord has placed within us not only the capacity for obedience, but also the potential to rebel. We may shake our fist against Him if we so choose. We see this principle and the outworking of it in the Garden of Eden where the Lord placed the tree of life along with the tree of the knowledge of good and evil. Adam and Eve were given the opportunity to choose. Therefore, when we submit ourselves in obedience to the Lord, we are not responding as puppets; but rather, out of a willing desire and love for Him. We have within us this power of choice.

For example, at times we may not feel like worshiping the Lord. But during these times, as we bend our will and give to Him our sacrifice of praise, our worship is especially received and appreciated by the Lord. Usually it is after an act of obedience such as this that the Lord will pour out His grace upon us, and an overflow of blessing will emerge.

This can be applied to any facet of our lives where obedience is required by the Lord. Yet if we look only toward the reward, we miss something. We must press on, knowing what the Word says. For it is in the sufferings of the refiner's fire that the pure gold, His Divine nature, is brought forth in our lives.

The Lord has shown us how this is to be accomplished. "*If anyone desires to come after Me, let him deny himself and take up his cross and follow Me.*" What is this cross, and how do we take it up?

> "For the flesh lusteth against the Spirit, and the Spirit against the flesh. And these are contrary (they *cross* †)

> the one to the other, so that ye cannot do the things that ye would" Gal 5:17 KJV (comment added).

There is an ongoing warfare, a struggle between our *natural* desires and His *spiritual* desire for us. Thus, there are two contrary wills at war with each other—"I will" and "Thy will." When the "Thy will" *(His purpose for us)* is contrary to and crosses out the "I will" *(our own wants)*, our cross is formed.

As I die to my own will, and then submit to and come into alignment with His will for me, I am indeed taking up my cross, thereby becoming one with Him.

I am to rise above all self-centered, self-seeking feelings and apply these to the cross that I might fully submit to the outworking of His will for me. I then become an upright, fruit-bearing branch on the tree of life, as a reflection, or extension of His life and purpose. I am doing as He would do.

The Apostle Paul cried from the depths of his being,

> "Not as though I had already attained, either were already perfect, but I am pressing on, if I may lay hold of that for which I also was taken hold of by Christ Jesus" Phil 3:12.

Notice that Paul said, "*if I may lay hold of.*" He understood that he had a choice to make.

We too have a responsibility to apply the cross to the very root of our self life; the totality of all that we are, and all that we desire to be, that we might fully follow Him.

> "The Kingdom of Heaven is taken by violence, and the violent take it by force" Matt 11:12b.

There is a spiritual battle to be won in entering the Kingdom realm. Those who truly love the Lord, and who desire to be rightly related to Him in His Kingdom will press through.

The most important time for us in all of eternity is "the present moment." We are making choices and decisions today that will effect our eternal position and reward. Eternal life is not future; we have that now as part of our redemption. WHAT (not where) we will be in eternity will be the result of the accumulated choices and decisions which we are making—now.

Our "*new creation life*" is as a "seed" that has been deposited within us, which is presently being formulated and developed into completeness. When eventually it is released into the "soil" of eternity, it will unfold into full view, revealing what it had become during our present life experience.

Any seed when planted, grows to express its particular nature. We need not add anything to it, but simply expose it to the right elements. Then it will develop into the fullness of what it is. The extent to which we spiritually develop in the "here and now" will become our "measured state" *(thirty, sixty, or one hundred fold)* for all eternity.

Our present life primarily involves the formulation of this seed *(our spiritual development)*, through the outworking of our willing obedience to Him, overcoming by taking up our cross daily.

Then, when we find ourselves in the "atmosphere of eternity," the life that had been developed within this "seed" will be released into its full expression in His eternal presence and purpose.

The promise of the Lord is "*To him that overcometh.*" As we overcome through our willing obedience to the Lord, He will bring into our life experience this "good land" and provide the atmosphere to fertilize and water the "soil" of our obedience. This will prepare us for the coming harvest when that which we have become will be lifted up from the earth into His higher purpose.

> "The willing and the obedient shall eat the good of the land."

We must allow this process to find its full outworking in each of our lives. Then, when we stand before Him in eternity, He will look upon each of us and give us a new name, according to what He sees.

Chapter 12

The Process of Spiritual Growth

When Jesus spoke to His disciples, He often used expressions that were familiar to them.

> "Now as He walked by the sea of Galilee, He saw Simon and Andrew his brother casting a net into the sea: for they were fishers. And Jesus said unto them, Come ye after Me, and I will make you to become fishers of men. And straightway they forsook their nets, and followed Him" Mark 1:16-18 KJV.

Jesus had said, "*I have called you to a higher vocation.* You will continue to fish, but rather than fishing for fish, you will fish for men." Simon and Andrew were about to be lifted from one dimension of their life experience into a higher calling and purpose.

It may be that we fail to recognize the voice of the Lord because we expect Him to speak to us with a King James vocabulary, or we are satisfied with the "word" we receive through the ministry of personal prophecy. It is important that we listen for His voice in the everyday circumstances of our lives.

For example, many years ago, when a heavy rain began to fall, a farmer went into a shed to wait out the storm. As he looked out at the rows of corn, the Lord caused him to consider the nature of corn and his understanding was opened regarding the spiritual message that corn portrays.

The farmer's thoughts then turned to the parable of the sower concerning seed that is sown into different types of soil (Matt 13:3-23). A detailed comparison between this passage of Scripture and the corn in his field formed within him; and a ministry was birthed with five messages about corn which portrayed the path to spiritual maturity. He spent his remaining years ministering about corn with outstanding results.

One observation about corn is that it is golden in color. Gold speaks of the "divine nature" that is within the redeemed earthen vessels that we are.

> "I counsel you to buy from me gold tried in the fire, so that you may be rich; and white clothing, so that you may be clothed, and so that the shame of your nakedness does not appear" Rev 3:18a.

When we confess our sin and accept the cleansing power of the blood of Jesus, we are "justified" and declared to be righteous. Through redemption and Holy Spirit regeneration, we become a new creation and receive a new nature.

> "Through which He has given to us exceedingly great and precious promises, so that by these you might be partakers of the divine nature, having escaped the corruption that is in the world through lust" II Peter 1:4.

> "So that if any one is in Christ, that one is a new creature; old things have passed away; behold, all things have become new" II Cor 5:17.

Beginning as a spiritual baby, we are to grow into spiritual maturity, or adulthood. Salvation is a free gift, but spiritual maturity must be attained. We are not to remain as naked new-born spiritual babies, but we are to grow into spiritual maturity.

> "Desire the sincere milk of the Word, as newborn babes, so that you may grow by it" I Peter 2:2.

Jesus compared this "divine nature" to a seed being sown into fertile soil,

> "But he that received seed into the good ground is he that heareth the Word, and understandeth it; which also beareth fruit, and bringeth forth, some an hundredfold, some sixty, some thirty" Matt 13:23 KJV.

Just as this treasure of His divine nature is hidden within our earthen vessels, golden corn is hidden within a covering, with a tassel of hair on top. There is a distinct gradation in ears of corn. That is, not all ears of corn come to the same level of growth, or maturity. Likewise, our spiritual growth as a Christian follows a progressive development with comparable results.

> "Behold, the sower went out to sow" Matt 13:3b.

The intention of the sower is to reap an abundant harvest from the seed which he has sown. The condition of the soil has much to do with this harvest.

> "And as he sowed, some seeds fell by the wayside, and the birds came and devoured them. Some fell on stony places, where they did not have much earth. And they sprang up immediately, because they had no deepness of earth. And the sun rising, they were scorched, and because they had no root, they withered away. And some fell among thorns. And the thorns sprung up and choked them. And some fell on the good ground and yielded fruit, indeed one a hundredfold, and one sixty, and one thirty" Matt 13:4-8.

The seed that fell on the surface of this hardened soil (*wayside*) was eaten by the birds. Some had sprung up and withered because it was unable to take root *(stony places)*. Other seed had started to grow but was choked *(thorns)*. From these, there was no harvest. But the seed that fell into fertile soil produced a harvest that was either thirty, sixty, or one-hundred fold in its increase.

So also, the Lord "sows" His divine nature within the babe in Christ, intending it to develop into full maturity. He uses this parable to teach us that the rate of our spiritual growth is conditional rather than fixed. Therefore, our spiritual growth will be greatly hindered when the "soil" of our heart has not been properly prepared.

Thus, the seed of the Kingdom may fall on the "wayside" *(any spiritual indifference that has not been dealt with)*, or in the "stony places" *(the carnality we permit in our life experience)*, or it may fall among "thorns" *(critical attitudes)*. These result in spiritual poverty.

But when this same seed has been sown into "good soil" *(the inner being of one who maintains a quality prayer life, is spiritually hungry, and is obedient to His will)*, it will yield an abundant spiritual harvest.

In northern climates we experience an early Fall. At the first indication of a frost, we pick the green tomatoes from our gardens and place them on a window sill where the sun can shine on them. Here, they will gradually ripen and turn bright red. However, if some partially mature corn is placed on the same window sill, it will only dry out and become hard. This thirty-fold corn will not become sixty, or one hundred-fold corn.

So it is in the life of a Christian. Many Christians have the mistaken idea that they will be changed "on the way up." They imagine that they will depart from this earth realm as a babe in Christ, and arrive in heaven as a matured saint. But once our life has been lifted from the "soil" of His dealings, no further maturing is possible. It is too late, for like the ear of corn, no further change will take place.

Spiritually speaking, we are not tomatoes. Rather, we are as these ears of corn. Our spiritual development must come while our "roots" are in the ground of our present environment.

There is a limited time for the completion of this process of maturing spiritually. Just as the ear of corn must come to maturity during the growing season while its roots are within the soil, so there must be a proper response to the workings of the Lord within us during our life time. Then that which we have become will be lifted into His presence, where it will continue to unfold and expand throughout the eternal ages.

> "To him who overcomes I will grant to sit with Me in My Throne, even as I also overcame, and have sat down with My Father in His Throne" Rev 3:21.

Jesus qualified for His place in the Throne with His Father by overcoming the hindrances in His path.

> "Though being a Son, yet He learned obedience by the things which He suffered. And being made perfect, He became the Author of eternal salvation to all those who obey Him" Heb 5:8-9.

Now He is able to say to us, "*You are to overcome in the same way that I overcame.*"

In using the terms of their vocation to speak to Simon and Andrew, there was the danger that they would not hear as Jesus intended. He did not say to them, "*Follow me and fish for men.*" Rather, Jesus used terms that they understood to speak to them about a process that would qualify them for a higher vocation.

> "Come ye after me, and I will make you TO BECOME fishers of men" Mark 1:17b KJV.

We must "come" *(our attitude and desire)* to the "place" *(good ground)* where He will be able to bring about the changes within us that will qualify us to fish for men, rather than for fish.

> "For we are His workmanship, created in Christ Jesus to good works, which God has before ordained that we should walk IN them" Eph 2:10.

The *"good ground"* is soil that has been "turned" by the divine plow. This plow overturns our own ways to expose all that would hinder our spiritual growth.

The seed that fell into the *"wayside soil"* avoided the furrow in which He works. Our natural reaction is to step aside when we see this divinely appointed plow coming towards us. The dilemma we face as this plow digs into the furrow of our lives is that it will turn everything upside down, exposing the problems and hurts that we had carefully buried deep within us.

If we are willing to humble ourselves by dying to our pride and letting others see us as we really are, the Lord will change us at the very root of our being. Then the unhindered seed of the Kingdom will be able to grow into full maturity and bring forth an abundant harvest; thirty, sixty, and on to one-hundred fold.

Our new nature, grown to full maturity and ready to enter a cooperative relationship with Him, is the "product" that the Lord desires to harvest out of the "good soil" into which we have been sown.

> "Come, my beloved, let us go out into the field; let us stay in the villages. Let us rise up early to the vineyards; let us see if the vine flowers, whether the tender grape appears, and the pomegranates bud forth: there will I give thee My loves" SS 7:11-12.

In anticipation of biting into a fully formed golden

ear of corn, should I find it had only come to a thirty-fold completion in its development, I would be truly disappointed.

So also, the Lord greatly desires to bring us to full maturity in Him. Then, in that day, when we are lifted out of our present "covering," we will be found by Him to be a fully formed, one-hundred fold representation of the Lord Jesus Christ.

Chapter 13

A Small Beginning

"Behold, the sower went out to sow"
Matt 13:3b.

To those who have an "inner" ear to hear, the 13th chapter of Matthew reveals the foundational principles of the operation of the Kingdom of God.

> "When anyone hears the Word of the kingdom" Matt 13:19a.

Our participation in the Kingdom of God begins with our submission to the rule of the Throne of God over our lives, and over all that pertains to us.

> "For the Kingdom of God is not eating and drinking; but righteousness and peace and joy in the Holy Spirit" Rom 14:17.

> "For the Kingdom of God is not in word, but in power" I Cor 4:20.

> "Neither shall they say, Lo here! or, lo there! for, behold, the Kingdom of God is within you" Luke 17:21 KJV.

For the natural man, the "throne" that controls his life experience is a "self-centeredness" which caters to his physical needs, emotions, and desires.

For the one who has been born from above, the "self-life" that sits on this throne must be crucified and committed to the grave. Then, all control of our daily life experience is to be transferred to the higher "Throne" and placed under the governmental rule of the Kingdom of God.

To the extent that this transfer has taken place *(good ground)*, the fruit of the Kingdom *(righteousness, peace, and joy)* will be evident. Where there is any amount of mixture, *(wayside, stony places, thorns)*, the results are partial, and the effectual working of the power of the Kingdom will be hindered and limited.

> "And as he sowed, some seeds fell by the wayside, and the birds came and devoured them. Some fell on stony places, where they did not have much earth. And they sprang up immediately, because they had no deepness of earth: and the sun rising, they were scorched, and because they had no root, they withered away. And some fell among thorns. And the thorns sprung up and choked them. And some fell on the good ground and yielded fruit, indeed one an hundredfold, and one sixty, and one thirty" Matt 13:4-8

The "seed" that our Heavenly Father sows is "The Word of the Kingdom."

> "When anyone hears the Word of the Kingdom and does not understand it, then the wicked one comes and catches away that which was sown in his heart" Matt 13:19a.

It is important for us to notice and consider that it is impossible for this Seed of the Kingdom *(our total submission to His governmental rule)* to mature when it is sown in the wayside, stony places, or among thorns *(a life where there is mixture)*. Any initial acceptance of the Kingdom will be devoured, wither away, or it will be choked.

This seed of the Kingdom can only germinate and grow in "good ground."

Within this seed is all that is required for our participation with Him in His coming Kingdom rule. The "soil" into which it is sown is our commitment and submission to Him, as our Lord. Thus, it is extremely important that we both maintain and increase the quality of our spiritual life, that the potential within this seed may fully develop and mature.

In Matthew 13:31, we are told that this seed of the Kingdom is like *a grain of mustard seed*, which is the least of all seeds. Here, the Lord is telling us that the important thing is not the amount of spiritual capacity we have, but rather, how we value and apply what we have, no matter how small it may be.

Likewise, this *grain of mustard seed* tells us that the Lord begins with the minute spiritual potential that is within us, and seeks to develop this, rather than placing any emphasis on our natural talents or abilities.

> "And Moses was learned in all the wisdom of the Egyptians, and was mighty in words and in deeds . . . and seeing one being wronged, he defended him, and . . . struck the Egyptian. For he thought his brothers would understand that God would give them deliverance by his hand. But they did not understand . . . and Moses fled" Acts 7:22,24,25,29a.

Moses was highly trained in the ways of the world of his day. When he attempted to use this ability, he utterly failed and fled into the wilderness where, unknown to him, the Lord had prepared the circumstances that would be used to bring him to the end of his natural ability. Then the Lord waited for all this ability to be dissipated.

In Egypt, Moses had much to say, but in the wilderness there was no one to hear his "learned" sayings. Gradually, Moses wore down and wore out. Finally, he turned aside to "*a bush that burned with fire, but was not consumed*" (Exodus 3:2). Here, the eternal "I AM" spoke into Moses the "seed" that would develop until he was fully qualified to bring all of Israel out from Egyptian bondage and oppression.

Each one of us is uniquely called to function in a particular place for a particular purpose. Before the Lord can equip us in His ways, we must be brought to the end of our own ways. Therefore, there is a "divine arrangement" *(wilderness)* prepared for each of us—and the Lord is there, waiting for us to arrive.

The outworking of this may take a considerable amount of time. In the case of Moses, it took forty years. We do not have that much time, thus it is important that we learn from the mistakes of others, and quickly submit ourselves to the Lord, and to His Kingdom rule.

> "But now God has set the members, each one of them, in the body, as it has pleased Him" I Cor 12:18.

Once we are fully committed, the Lord can plant us in the type of "soil" *(wilderness)* that is needed to develop the seed He has sown within us. Left to ourselves, we would seek an easier place or way, and as a result, the potential within us would come short of its full development.

Each one of us is presently in one of two situations. Either we have been firmly planted by the Lord in the soil of our present circumstances, or the Lord is seeking to lead us to the place *(soil)* of His choosing. He is well able, if necessary *(as in the case of Moses)*, to make an arrangement from which we will flee into the center of His will *(our wilderness)* for the necessary time of preparation.

> "For it under his direction that the whole body is perfectly adjusted and united by every joint that furnishes its supplies; and by the proper functioning of each particular part, there is brought about the growing of the body for its building up in love" Eph 4:16 Williams.

Our lives are affected by others. Church members especially have a way of perfecting each other. We have a tendency to seek a way of escape from our present circumstances in order to find an easier arrangement in which to live and function. It is important that each one of us abide where the Lord has "sown" us—even if it is in the midst of those whom He has appointed to "reduce" us.

After forty years, Moses came to the place where he recognized that his own ways were not adequate.

> "And Moses said unto the Lord, O my LORD, I am not eloquent, neither heretofore, nor since thou hast spoken unto thy servant: but I am slow of speech, and of a slow tongue" Exodus 4:10 KJV.

It was not that he was unable to speak, but now he realized that when he had much to say, he accomplished little. In fact, it brought him trouble from which he fled. Now Moses has come to know that he is not to speak unless the Lord give him the words. Therefore, he asked for a prophet, Aaron, to speak in his behalf.

The Lord may not assign a prophet to each of us, but He will make us "prophetic" that we might cooperate with Him in the development of the potential *(seed)* that has been sown within us. As the grain of mustard seed buried within us develops, the Kingdom of God will find its initial expression, as we are brought into divine order and function.

> "And it shall come to pass in the last days, saith God, I will pour out of my Spirit upon all flesh: and your sons and your daughters shall prophesy, and your young men shall see visions, and your old men shall dream dreams: and on my servants and on my handmaidens I will pour out in those days of my Spirit; and they shall prophesy" Acts 2:17-18 KJV.

This speaks of a prophetic anointing which the Lord will impart and develop within His servants during the last days. To prophesy, one must be prophetic, which means, a prophetic quality has been developed within.

How does this take place? *"A sower went forth to SOW . . . THE WORD of the Kingdom."* Jesus said that this seed is the least of all seeds. Thus, although I may feel inadequate to prophesy, I can make provision *(prepare the soil)* in which this prophetic "seed" is to grow. To do this, I abide where the "Son" may continually shine upon me. I receive the "rain" of the Holy Spirit and give it time to soak within. I listen attentively for His voice, ready to respond and obey.

We are to "*desire spirituals*" (I Cor 14:1). This exhortation goes beyond our seeking the gifts of the Spirit. It tells us that we are to desire the **realm** of the Spirit. In this realm of the Spirit, we are lifted from the temporal into the eternal, from the carnal into the spiritual.

When I first enter this realm, the "prophetic" grain of mustard seed that has been sown within me will appear to be small and insignificant, in comparison to my "natural" abilities of expression, which predominate and usually are well developed. Therefore, it will require a "fasting" *(time in the wilderness)* to bring this natural ability to its end. Fasting is more than skipping meals. There is a fasting from words, from having a quick opinion or answer. There are those who instantly have something to say about everything. Fasting will bring this to an end. It will bring us to silence until God speaks.

> "Follow after love and desire spirituals so that you might prophesy" I Cor 14:1 (literal translation).

Our Lord is calling a people to become prophetic, that the whole Body will be built together and compacted by that which every joint supplies. Only then will the Kingdom of God become a present reality.

Chapter 14

Steps Toward A Spirit-Led Life

"If we live in the Spirit, let us also walk in the Spirit"
Gal 5:25

Many of us desire to live a Spirit-led life. To do so means that we have died to our own ways, submitted ourselves to the governmental rule of His Kingdom, and have given to the Lord the unconditional right to choose for us. We are to walk as He would walk.

> "Thy kingdom come, Thy will be done in *(our)* earth, as it is in heaven" Matt 6:10 KJV (Comment added).

The ability to continually walk in the Spirit, in which His will is being done in our earth, requires that we have a basic understanding of the laws that govern a Spirit-led life. More difficult, it necessitates an abiding, unquestioning, submission to the government of His Kingdom. Therefore, along with a committed daily walk of being led by His Spirit, this submission to His Kingdom rule includes our acceptance of the preparatory teachings and the practical disciplines that are laid upon us by the Lord.

The purpose of these is to produce within us an increasing sensitivity to the voice of the Holy Spirit, and an enlarging of our willingness and ability to understand and cooperate with His leadings and movings.

The Kingdom of God is a realm in which there is much activity, but where everything moves in divine order and purpose. A baby walks falteringly for a few steps and falls; his direction is arbitrary and casual. A child walks for his own enjoyment and amusement. A young man walks to attain his goals and fulfill his visions. A father walks to please and satisfy the needs of his family. He has a higher purpose than his own satisfaction.

This involves spiritual perception, dedication, and sacrificial giving. These are marks of maturity. It is the same in the realm and program of the Kingdom. As babes in Christ, we must develop spiritually before we can begin to intelligently walk in the Spirit. This involves a total commitment to the Lord. The schoolmaster and teacher for this processing is the Holy Spirit. We must enroll in this school of training and preparation if we are to receive its benefits. The Registrar is always available.

To walk in the Spirit is to walk one step at a time, acknowledging His headship and presence each step that we take. Our own thoughts and ways must be set aside in order to follow Him. He is the Christ, the Anointed of the Lord. Therefore, the natural man cannot come this way, for he cannot discern the presence, or the anointing that brings one into this higher realm, for it is a function of the Spirit, not of the mind.

The children of Israel were to abide under the pillar of fire by night and the cloud by day. They were to move only as the pillar of fire or the cloud moved. The purpose of this discipline was to teach them the importance of being led by His Spirit. Had they learned and obeyed, Israel would have won one victory after another in possessing the land, and would have become the witness and forerunner of the Theocratic Kingdom that the Lord desired to establish in the earth.

The Lord greatly desires to introduce us to His Kingdom through a Spirit-led life and walk. He cannot allow us to have a part in this higher governmental realm of His Kingdom until we have individually, unconditionally, submitted our lives to be governed by Him, and have in some measure, learned how to *"walk in the Spirit."*

Certain basic principles must be understood in seeking this higher realm of His Kingdom and a Spirit-led life.

> The term "flesh" is the name given to the natural state and activity of man, independent of and uncontrolled by, the Holy Spirit.

> The terms, led by; moved by; walking in the Spirit; are names of the supernatural state and activity of man, totally dependent upon and totally controlled by the Holy Spirit.

The above conditions are contrary to each other, yet so similar in action that spiritual perception is required to recognize the transition from one realm into the other. Man's spirit and soul are so closely allied that it takes the living Word of God to distinguish one from the other. God has sent His Spirit to accomplish this. The original divine purpose was to make of man a being that lived and moved in complete harmony and unity with God.

In the first test, man utterly failed and fell into the lower realm of flesh life. Through the life, death, and resurrection of Jesus Christ, a way back to this higher realm of spirit life has been established and the way of entrance set before us.

In the past, our spiritual comprehension has been dull and our progress toward this higher realm slow. Therefore, "the Baptism in the Holy Spirit and Fire" has been made available as the means to enable us to enter this realm of spiritual life and reality—His Kingdom. With many, this experience has fallen into a lower realm of "blessing" rather than being the "enabling" that would lead into this higher realm of spiritual life and purpose.

Many are satisfied with receiving the spiritual blessings and imparted gifts of the enabling, rather than seeking after "the enduement of power" that would bring us into this higher realm. It is important for us to understand this experience of being "Baptized in the Holy Spirit" in the right perspective, as a greater intervention of God is upon us in these last days. The Holy Spirit is marvelously moving upon many with the intention of bringing them up into this higher realm.

Paul prayed, "*The eyes of your understanding being enlightened; that you may know what is the hope of His calling, and what is the riches of the glory of His inheritance in the saints*" Eph 1:18. There is much available that we have yet to appropriate, but we are settling for less than His adequate provision.

Our Lord is challenging us to move upward and onward. The present dissatisfaction and searching within the Body of Christ is His prodding. The "movings" of the Holy Spirit within and upon us are His means. The Kingdom of God is His goal.

For us to "Walk in the Spirit" is to become a subject of His Kingdom. Let us move upward as we walk with Him.

Chapter 15

The Submission Of Our Rights

"And a great multitude followed Him, because they saw His miracles which He did on them that were diseased"
John 6:2 KJV.

These came as observers. Jesus multiplied five loaves and two fishes until this entire multitude of more than five thousand men, women, and children had been fed to the full. They were looking to be blessed, and were therefore fed on the level of their interest.

When they returned seeking another meal, Jesus spoke a word of correction to them. He said the "food" they should be seeking was on a higher level and then left them. Later, He again responded to their need, but this time openly offered them that which was of eternal value.

> "I am the Living Bread which came down from Heaven. If anyone eats of this Bread, he shall live forever. And truly the bread that I will give is My flesh, which I will give for the life of the world. Then the Jews argued with one another, saying, How can this man give us his flesh to eat?" John 6:51-52.

They had readily received and ate the multiplied loaves and fishes and then returned, asking for more; yet when Jesus offered His very life to them, they rejected Him. They did not have a spiritual "ear" to hear, or the capacity to receive what He offered. Therefore, they nullified a choice opportunity for a teaching that would have prepared (conditioned) them to receive the True Bread of Heaven.

> "From this time many of His disciples went back into the things behind, and walked no more with Him" John 6:66.

Today, as then, there is an urgent need for foundational teaching concerning a deeper life commitment to the Lord. An upwardly directed spirit is essential if there is to be within us any receptivity and understanding on the deeper levels of spiritual life.

> "He answered and said to them, Because it is given to you to know the mysteries of the kingdom of Heaven, but it is not given to them" Matt 13:11.

The ability to "hear" the true message of the Kingdom is given to us as a result of our submission to a "conditioning" process. Only when we have fully yielded the totality of our being to the work of the cross and have a determination of heart to go further, will there be within us the quality of spirit that will enable us to respond to His deeper working in our lives.

This spiritual capacity can only be developed within the privacy of a "heart level" submission to the hand of the Lord upon our lives. This may be a problem to some, as it is beyond the ability of our mental understanding and requires of us a blind commitment and trust. Therefore, there may be some inward wrestling and struggling before we will be able to unconditionally submit all to the Lord and begin to partake of His life.

It is not expected at this point that we will be fully able to keep this commitment, but only that we make it with a determination to unreservedly submit ourselves to Him. This heart determination will find its outworking through our submission to the desire of Jesus to take us further. We do this by going beyond the receiving of "loaves and fishes" by unconditionally making Him "Lord" of our lives and partaking of His very life.

> "He who partakes of My flesh and drinks My blood dwells in Me and I in him. As the living Father has sent Me, and I live through the Father, so he who partakes of Me, even he shall live by Me" John 6:56-57.

At times, we may feel un-spiritual and defeated due to lingering problems. All the Lord seeks is entrance that He may become personally known to us. As we respond to Him, our problems will fade into a singular desire to truly know Him and partake of His life. All else will proceed from this, as our love for Him and a longing to be with Him develops.

A lasting commitment of this depth can rarely be made during the time that we are stirred by an emotional message, or by an intense altar call. Rather, it must be done when we are alone with the Lord, where we can search our heart's desires and intentions, and then submit the totality of our being to Jesus— all that we are along with all that we ever hope to be— and lay all this at His feet, making Him our Lord and placing Him in full control of our lives.

We must give Him specific permission to change us, and then cooperate with Him as He accomplishes this. This means that He will initiate a set of circumstances which are designed to bring about the necessary changes that will make us conformable to the image of the Lord Jesus Christ (Rom 8:29) and equip us for His purposes.

> "For it is God who works in you both to will and to do of His good pleasure" Phil 2:13.

The Lord will quietly continue this "life changing" work within us, causing us "*to will and do His good pleasure.*" If we begin to deviate in any way from His workings within us, an inner voice will quietly say, "no." These "checks" of the Holy Spirit are to be greatly valued and explicitly obeyed.

> "And your ears shall hear a word behind you, saying, This is the way, walk in it, when you turn to the right hand, and when you turn to the left" Isaiah 30:21.

As we rightly respond, we will begin to feel the strength, security, and blessing of being under His control and protection. As we continue, we will recognize that we were made for this and that we should have begun much sooner.

When we make Jesus "Lord" of our lives, we place ourselves on "Kingdom ground" where the Holy Spirit is free to either "quicken us" in confirmation, or to "check us" when we turn aside. This ability to respond to His quickening presence for "guidance" will increase as we respond in obedience and cultivate our sensitivity to His abiding presence.

Only as we separate ourselves from the things that could pull us down and hinder our spiritual walk, and then discipline our lives to obey His voice will this be accomplished.

> "The light of the body is the eye. Therefore, if your eye is sound, your whole body shall be full of light. But if your eye is evil, your whole body shall be full of darkness. If therefore the light that is in you is darkness, how great is that darkness!" Matt 6:22-23.

Any carnal intrusion will become a hindrance to the "eye of the Lord" which guides us. All of these perverse, negative things must first be "washed" out of us so there will be room for Him when He comes to fellowship with us and work within us.

As we cultivate a keen, perceptive sensitivity to His presence, we will increasingly be able to cooperate with Him. This sensitivity to His presence does not just happen. It must be developed within. There is a cost, as it takes time for this level of spiritual maturity to develop.

As our spiritual appetites are deepened, we will reach beyond the loaves and fishes, and in anticipation, respond to His offer to partake of His flesh and of His blood, becoming one with Him in our being, and in all we do together with Him.

Chapter 16

Qualification for His Kingdom

"Go in through the narrow gate, for wide is the gate,
and broad is the way that leads to destruction,
and many there are who go in through it.
Because narrow is the gate and constricted is the way
which leads to life, and there are few who find it"
Matt 7:13-14.

Within Christianity is a difficult "narrow way" which leads to His highest. There is also an easy "broad way" which leads to the loss of His best for us. There is a "cost" to coming into all that the Lord intends.

Our Heavenly Father has predestinated us to be made conformable to the image of His Son, the Lord Jesus Christ. Jesus was in all points tempted like as we are, yet without sin (Heb 4:15). He became the first overcomer. Now, He can say to us,

> "To him who overcomes I will grant to sit with Me in My throne, even as I also overcame and have sat down with My Father in His throne" Rev 3:21.

As we overcome, we grow, and through "placement" we are set as members into the corporate Body of Christ that we are becoming.

> "But now God has set the members, each one of them, in the body as it has pleased Him. And if they were all one member, where would be the body? But now indeed many are the members, yet only one body" I Cor 12:18-20.

We then become a vital part, a member of a many membered body of which Jesus is the head.

> "And this until we all come into the unity of the faith and of the knowledge of the Son of God, to a full-grown man, to the measure of the stature of the fullness of Christ" Eph 4:13.

This "measure" means that we as "particular" members of His body, who have been born again as "babes in Christ," must grow up so this corporate Body that we are becoming will become proportionate to Jesus, the adult head.

Jesus fully obeyed His Father. On the Cross, having perfectly fulfilled His Father's will, He said, "*It is finished.*" Thus, Jesus as our corporate Head is a fully developed adult head.

We begin our spiritual journey as a born-again baby. Peter tells us,

> "As newborn babes, desire the pure milk of the Word, that you may grow thereby" I Peter 2:2 KJV.

We become a one-year-old, and on through the stages of growth toward spiritual maturity, until the corporate body of which we are a member has become rightly proportioned to the adult head, our Lord Jesus Christ. The Father, and all of creation, is waiting for this fully developed corporate Body.

> "For the earnest expectation of the creation waits for the manifestation of the sons of God" Rom 8:19.

Thus, the end of the Church age can come only when this corporate Body has grown into a level of spiritual maturity whereby it can be rightly joined to the Head and then manifested. The Father alone determines when this level of growth has been reached. This is not a pre-determined date, but rather the result of the development of the Body to the "measure" of the Head, our Lord Jesus Christ.

Jesus said, *"To him who overcomes I will grant to sit with Me in My throne . . ."* Not every Christian is an overcomer. Not every Christian grows to spiritual maturity. Only a Bride who has fully prepared Herself will sit with Him in His throne.

Thus, there is within the Church "a people within a people;" those who have given themselves to the full processings of the Father as "*His workmanship*" (Eph 2:10) that they might be brought into full maturity, "*to the measure of the stature of the fullness of Christ.*"

To become a partaker with Him in His Millennial reign is conditional.

> "And he who overcomes and keeps My works to the end, to him I will give power over the nations. And he will rule them with a rod of iron, as the vessels of a potter they will be broken to pieces, even as I received from My Father" Rev 2:26-27.

There are many Christians who do not measure up to the "condition" that is established in this passage of Scripture.

Revelation 5:6,8 speaks of "twenty-four elders" and "four living creatures" who are in the midst of the Throne. The twenty four elders are a type of those who have qualified as overcomers throughout the Old Testament. There were those such as Enoch, who "walked with God and was not." The twelve patriarchs became the twelve tribes of Israel. Twelve apostles became the foundation upon which the Church is built.

The "four living creatures" refer to the New Testament overcomer. They had the face of a lion, a calf, a man, and an eagle. These represent the four sides of a fully developed, overcoming life. The lion symbolizes spiritual authority; the calf, sacrifice or service; the man, fellowship; and the eagle, spirituality.

These, the four living creatures and the twenty-four elders fell down before the Lamb, each one having harps and golden vials full of incense, which are the prayers of saints,

> "And they sang a new song, saying, You are worthy to take the book, and to open its seals, for you were slain and have redeemed us to God by Your blood out of every kindred and tongue and people and nation. And You made us kings and priests to our God, and we shall reign over the earth" Rev 5:9-10.

These are the redeemed who have been taken from among every kindred, tongue, people, and nation, and perfectly fit the position of the overcomer in Rev 2:26 and Rev 3:21.

> "And he who overcomes and keeps My works to the end, to him I will give power over the nations" Rev 2:26.

> "To him who overcomes I will grant to sit with me in My throne, even as I also overcame and have sat down with My Father in His throne" Rev 3:21.

Notice Rev 19:7-8 in the New American Standard translation,

> "Let us rejoice and be glad and give the glory unto Him, for the marriage of the Lamb has come and His bride has made herself ready. And it was given to her to clothe herself in fine linen, bright and

clean; for the fine linen is the righteous acts of the saints."

This passage clearly identifies the Bride with those who have become "overcomers."

Ephesians 2:8-9 tells us, "*For by grace you are saved through faith, and that not of yourselves, it is the gift of God. Not of works, lest anyone should boast.*" Salvation is a gift, but once we are saved we have a part in the preparation process of our spiritual growth. "*His Bride has made herself ready.*"

There is the garment of salvation, white and clean (Rev 7:13-14). Also, there is the garment of the Bride, who has arrayed herself in fine linen, which is the righteous (overcoming) acts of the saints. Thus, the one who came to the marriage feast with only a "salvation garment" was cast out (Matt 22:11-14).

The five wise virgins entered through the door, but to the foolish virgins, the door was shut. All ten had the garment of salvation, but only the wise had the garment of the overcomer (Bride).

In Rev 5:9-10, a group from every kindred, tongue, people, and nation are singing and saying, "*You have made us unto our God kings and priests, and we shall reign on the earth.*" In Rev 7:9-15 is seen a multitude from all nations, kindreds, people, and tongues. These are "before" the throne having a white robe and palms in their hands, crying with a loud voice saying, "*Salvation.*" These serve Him day and night in His temple.

Our testimony identifies our "position" with the Lord. In Revelation 5:9, the "overcomers" were singing. In Rev 7:10, those who were "before" the throne were crying. The group in Rev 5:10 (the five wise virgins) had become kings and priests and were "reigning." The second group in Rev 7:15 (the five foolish virgins) were saved, but had gone no further and were "serving."

These (the second group) were satisfied to wash their robes in the blood of Jesus to gain entrance to heaven. The Lord will wipe away their tears, but they will never partake with Him in His Throne. There is a difference.

What is it that makes this difference? It is our commitment and our obedience. If we are satisfied to live merely as a carnal Christian, we will find ourselves standing before the throne at the end of time, crying "salvation." This will be all we have.

Only those who make Him Lord and fully commit their lives to Him, will have a part with Him in the Millennial Kingdom. It is not His intention that any one of us should come short of this. The choice is ours to make.

"For many are called, but few chosen" Matt 22:14.

There is something more to gain than Heaven.

Chapter 17

The Purpose of His Dealings

When we place ourselves under the headship of the Lord as our Father, and submit our lives unconditionally to His governmental Kingdom rule, the Lord will begin to intervene in our attitudes and in all we do, with correction.

If this process of "chastening correction" is presently taking place within your life, it is because you have given the Lord the right to do so, and you are cooperating with Him as He intervenes for our well-being. Take a few moments and ask yourself this question. "Do I know the Lord as a Father who in love, is chastening and correcting me?"

> "For whom the Lord loves He chastens, and He scourges every son whom He receives. If you endure chastening, God deals with you as with sons, for what son is he whom the father does not chasten?" Heb 12:6-7.

Our being "dealt" with by the Lord may sometimes seem to us as being like a bad word; something that we should avoid. This reaction comes because of a fear that our being "dealt with" may deprive us of relationships we desire, things we want, or places we wish to go.

However, the dealings of the Lord are always creative and positive. From an eternal perspective, they will leave us much better off than we had been. Their purpose is not to put us down, but rather to lift us up. Being dealt with is not "some terrible thing" that is happening to us, but rather involves the Lord removing the bad, along with some "seemingly" some good things, so He might give us better things. Furthermore, these better things are lined up, waiting. Thus, His dealings are not bad—they are a blessing, and should be welcomed. Once we have experienced this, we will actually welcome His correction.

The Lord's dealings and scourgings affect us in three basic areas of our spiritual experience.

The first relates to the cross; the taking up of "our" cross by denying our self life with all of its desires and ambitions.

> "Then Jesus said to His disciples, If anyone desires to come after Me, let him deny himself and take up his cross and follow Me. For whoever desires to save his life shall lose it, and whoever desires to lose his life for My sake shall find it" Matt 16:24-25.

"Denying self" means that I am choosing the Lord and His ways. I am establishing Him as my Head, thereby allowing all decisions to come from Him. To do this, I must commit all that relates to "my head" (my own ways) to the cross. As I rightly respond to this process and die to these things upon the cross that I take up, I rise above all self motivation and gratification —up above my earthly desires, I OVERcome.

There are critical "testing" points concerning this decision by which the "things" I desire become a cross. These are designed to deal with the root of my self life. Once this "root" has been weakened and finally severed, it becomes increasingly easier to respond in obedience to the Lord.

Many are suspicious that the Lord may be trying to do them in, or that He is seeking to deprive them of something they feel they should have. This is the point that Satan made with Eve, when he provoked her to transgress the Word of the Lord. But as we grow in our obedience to the Lord, we discover that when these desires and things are crucified upon the cross, we are far better off, because we had said "yes" and allowed the Lord to do it His way.

Had we gone our own way, it would have become a process of death working within us, which would have robbed us of all that the Lord intended for us.

Even though we may presently feel differently, down the road, we will see in a far greater perspective the results of His dealings in our lives and we will begin to understand and rejoice. Once we discover that He indeed knew better all the time, we will love the Lord as never before with a deep and trusting love, and it will become progressively easier for us to say "Yes, Lord" and take up our cross and follow Him.

The second area in which the Lord is dealing with us is to bring us into an "overcoming" relationship with Himself.

> "To him who overcomes I will grant to sit with Me in My throne, even as I overcame and have sat down with My Father in His throne" Rev 3:21.

"*To him who overcomes.*" To be seated with Jesus in His throne is conditional. Therefore, it is not available to all Christians, but only to those who, through a process of testing and proving, have overcome.

To become an overcomer, there must be something to overcome. Often we will find that we are being challenged to overcome that which we intensely feel we must have or do. The Lord may draw a line through this desire and simply say "no." This "line" then becomes our "cross."

> "If anyone desires to come after Me, let him deny himself and take up (OVERcome) his cross, and follow Me."

At this point, either knowingly, or unconsciously, we determine whether the Lord is more important to us than the thing we desire. We must realize that the Lord longs to give good things to those who love Him. He is not depriving us, but there are certain "testing" points that we must successfully pass through in order to reach His best.

During our time of testing, we can rest in the fact that the Lord is able to take all things and make them "*work together for good.*" To overcome, we must make the right choice, which then becomes the foundation upon which He will bring the greater (unknown to us at the time) blessing.

The third area of dealings concerns our "words" to each other. This is extremely important, as victory in this area is a primary mark of spiritual maturity.

> "For in many things we all offend. If anyone does not offend in word, the same is a full-grown man, able also to bridle the whole body" James 3:2.

Some become confused or hurt through some opinion or advice they receive. If "advice" is received from six different people, all six pieces of advice will probably differ. We must be careful when giving advice that we share only that which the Lord is saying. Only then will all harmonize. Advice is easy to give; therefore, it is extremely important that we hear from the Lord before we express an opinion, or advise another.

Our relationships must first be established in the Lord *(we die to our feelings)*, so we may rightly share "His Word" *(not our opinions or reactions)* with one another. Each one of us should have much of the written Word resident within us through our "devotional" relationship to the Word of God. Then we can be quickened by the Holy Spirit to speak the Word of the Lord to those who are needy, at the time of their need. This is a practical "ministry" that often is not recognized. Our whole life is to be a witness and a testimony of the living Christ.

This will require of us a prophetic ability that will release a "word" that comes from the Lord, which we share as being precious, not just free advice. Because it comes from the Lord, we will be speaking the mind of Christ. If six different people were to function in this prophetic anointing, the same word would come from all six. When the Word of the Lord is rightly spoken, in the right place, at the right time, there will be no confusion, and no one will be hurt due to wrong advice or opinions.

This prophetic anointing will develop within us, as we are being changed through the "dealings" which the Lord has placed in our path. Any "ministry" that we attempt should begin after, not before, this time of testing and preparation. The Lord is pleased to bless us when our approach to Him follows "His ways."

It is important that we become prophetic, not just so we may prophesy. We are to become receptive and sensitive to the prophetic presence of the Lord. Then the words which we speak to one another will be the Words of the Lord.

Not everyone will fully submit themselves to His "dealings" in their lives, but those who have done so will be rewarded "in that day," when they stand tall before the Lord. The Father will take His "measuring stick" and measure Jesus; then He will measure us to see how we compare, and whether we have come "*to the measure of the stature of the fullness of Christ*" (Eph 4:13b).

If deep within us, we allow a desire "to do our own thing" to control us, and we ignore or reject His dealings, we will be robbed of the precious time that we have available to us in which to overcome and measure up to the "stature" of the Lord Jesus Christ. Then, when we stand before the Father to be "measured," we will have fallen short of His intention and purpose.

Today is our opportunity to face these tests, welcome His dealings, and become an OVERcomer.

Chapter 18

The Blessings of Adversity

"For we are His workmanship, created in Christ Jesus
to good works, which God has before ordained
that we should walk in them"
Eph 2:10.

The word "we" in this verse speaks of all who identify themselves with the Apostle Paul by willingly, unconditionally placing their lives in the hands of the Master Workman, our Heavenly Father. In this way, we are created (made available) unto good works.

The "*good works*" are those many varied circumstances that affect us each day of our lives, which are arranged and orchestrated by the Lord.

Some of these good works, however, may feel rough as sandpaper or sharp as a cutting instrument. Nevertheless, these difficult circumstances have a purpose. They are among the "tools" that our Heavenly Father uses in the process of making us conformable to the image of His Son, our Lord Jesus Christ.

Each one of us is individually known to the Lord. We are "*His workmanship.*" He knows when a sparrow falls to the ground; and He knows exactly where we are in our present life situation.

Many of us have said at one time or another, "If it were not for my present circumstances, I would be much more spiritual than I am now." Or, "I could do much better if I were in a different place." The Lord has a ready answer for us. During His time on earth, He lived among a people who were continually antagonistic toward Him, until they finally crucified Him. Yet He is able to say to us,

> "To him who overcomes I will grant to sit with Me in My throne, EVEN AS I ALSO OVERCAME, and have sat down with My Father in His throne" Rev 3:21.

Jesus always submitted to the will of His Father and never acted on His own. He faced the enemy in a barren wilderness after He had become intensely hungry, and under extreme pressure refused to eat until His Father had provided for Him.

When we complain to the Lord about our present situation, He will remind us that not only had He overcome under adverse circumstances, but He had placed Adam and Eve in a perfect environment within the Garden of Eden where their situation could not have been more desirable. The Lord had manifestly walked with them in the cool of each evening. Yet with all this available to them, they failed.

Thus, when we complain to the Lord that we would do much better if we were in a different environment, He will simply remind us that this has already been tried, but did not work.

According to the testimonies recorded in chapter eleven of Hebrews, and those of many overcomers since the day of Pentecost, multitudes have come to the

Lord's highest through times of adversity, suffering, and temptation. These became the tools that formed a people who truly knew the Lord. An on-going train of saints, having paid a price for their faith, live in His eternal presence while testifying of the quality *(His image)* that this "short moment" of adversity had produced within them.

That which the Lord could not get from man while he lived within the comforts of a garden of perfection, He is presently extracting through an environment that is far less than that. The enemy thought he had defeated God by deceiving Adam and Eve. Instead, he caused them to enter an environment wherein they (and us) could become overcomers.

To become an overcomer requires the presence of difficult, contrary situations that provide us with an opportunity to choose.

> "To him who overcomes I will grant to sit with Me in My Throne . . ."

All that the enemy was able to accomplish by causing Adam and Eve to be cast out of the Garden of Eden was to provide tools *(good works)* for the Master Workman to use in forming overcomers (us, if we rightly respond) into the mature image of our Lord Jesus Christ.

My first decision, after I settled the fact of being in the ministry, was to limit my ministry to an area within twenty miles of my home town. Shortly after this, the Lord caused me to understand that I was before Him as a small, tender plant that needed to grow. I saw that some plants grow best in a hot, tropical climate; others in a cool, northern climate.

I began to pray, "Lord, you know far better than I what kind of environment is needed that I might grow into the fullness of the potential that is within me. Lord, cause me to be planted in the climate *(good works)* that I need, wherever it may be."

Now, I was willing to go anywhere that the Lord might lead. I realized that I was His workmanship *(a tender plant)* and He, as the master Gardener, had prepared *(before ordained)* for me a series of circumstances (in this case, adverse and challenging) that would result in His satisfaction (joy) with the mature person I would become.

The Lord is waiting to roll up His sleeves and go to work. If we allow Him to re-form us as He chooses, using whatever "tools" He may deem necessary to accomplish His purpose, then in that day when we stand before Him, He will be able to say,

> "Well done, good and faithful servant! you have been faithful over a few things, I will make you ruler over many things. Enter into the joy of your Lord" Matt 25:21.

It is eternally important that first, we recognize and accept the fact that the Lord in His infinite wisdom and love, has placed *(before ordained)* us in our present environment—a "greenhouse" of His choosing, where we can become all that He intends us to be.

And then, we are to fully cooperate with Him in all that takes place in the outworking of this process.

Chapter 19

Attaining That Which Is Best

"That I may know Him, and the power of His
resurrection, and the fellowship of His sufferings,
being made conformable to His death.

If by any means I might attain unto the resurrection of
the dead. Not as though I had already attained, either were
already perfect: but I am pressing on, if I may lay hold of
that for which I also was taken hold of by Christ Jesus.

My brothers, I do not count myself to have taken
possession, but one thing I do, forgetting the things
behind, and reaching forward to the things before,

I press toward the mark for the prize of the
high calling of God in Christ Jesus"
Phil 3:10-14.

We must guard our spirits against all those things that can hinder the quality of our spiritual lives. Otherwise, our sensitivity to His presence, along with our understanding of spiritual principles, will become clouded and will begin to deteriorate.

As a result, we will be robbed of His best in our spiritual development. These negative influences, if not dealt with, will gradually undermine the progress we have made toward spirituality. As a result, we will begin to feel that the Lord is far away, and worse, not interested in us.

It is important that we actively both desire and value His presence. When we neglect to do our part in cultivating and maintaining an abiding sense of His presence in our daily lives, we will lose our sensitivity to spiritual things, as well as our interest in personally knowing the Lord.

If we are sincere in our desire for His best, all attachments that are not compatible with His will and purpose for us, along with those things that do not relate to His workings within us, must be brought to the cross and left there. We will recognize these as we put the Lord first in all that pertains to us and as we actively seek His will. Only then will a firm foundation be established upon which a lasting, abiding friendship with the Lord may be cultivated.

As we continue in our times of communion with the Lord, our perception and understanding of spiritual things will increase. We will become aware of an ever expanding spiritual capacity and desire to respond to Him, and we will place a greater value upon His abiding presence and workings within our lives. From day to day, we may not recognize this progression into increased spirituality, but nevertheless, it is taking place. At some point in time, we will come to know that we are not what we once were, but we will not understand how we got to where we are.

Consider the dealings in David's life as the Lord prepared him to be King over Israel in Saul's stead. A short time after he had been anointed by Samuel to be King, David was brought into the palace to serve Saul. During this time, as he played his harp before Saul,

David pondered the throne, and all that he hoped to accomplish when it became his.

During one of these times, Saul threw a javelin at David and ordered him killed. David fled into the wilderness with Saul's army in pursuit and hid in the back of a cave. As David faced death in the darkness of his place of hiding, all his dreams and ambitions concerning the throne of Israel lost their allure.

Now, nothing mattered but the Lord Himself. All that David had been concerned about suddenly was of no value. With this understanding, he fully submitted himself to the Lord and began to seek Him as never before. With this new sense of eternal values, David expressed his inner being to the Lord:

> "One thing I have desired from the Lord, that I will seek after; that I may dwell in the house of the Lord all the days of my life, to behold the beauty of the Lord, and to pray in His temple" Psalm 27:4.

David had been reduced to "*one thing*." Now the Lord was first in His life. The throne that emerged in the darkness of the cave was eternal—the throne of the King of kings. The throne of Israel no longer mattered.

The Lord's ways are far different than ours. While hiding in the back of a cave, David had been prepared to sit upon the throne of Israel. Now the Lord could trust him in places of pressure. He would not fail the Lord, as Saul had.

> "My son, despise not the chastening of the Lord, nor faint when you are rebuked by Him: For whom the Lord loves He chastens, and He scourges every son whom He receives" Heb 12:5b-6.

We are to put our faith in the Lord with a child like confidence that He is concerned about us. Realizing that the Lord has a before-determined plan and purpose for our lives, we can then trust Him to bring it about.

> "Truly I say to you, unless you are converted, and become as little children, you shall not enter into the kingdom of Heaven" Matt 18:3.

It will require a drastic reduction in our being before we will be able to lay aside all our aspirations and ideas, and in naked faith, trust the Lord, knowing that His way and that which He has for us, is far better than anything we could accomplish on our own.

There are those who have a pleasing personality, or have much natural ability, but many of us do not. Actually, those who are not gifted in these areas are better off as it is easier for them to trust the Lord. Thus, as we acknowledge our insufficiency to the Lord, we are affirming our dependence upon Him.

Paul learned how necessary it was to totally depend on the Lord.

> "Brethren, I count not myself to have apprehended: but this one thing I do, forgetting those things which are behind and reaching forth unto those things which are before" Phil 3:13 KJV.

He focused his vision in the right place.

We also are to cultivate this "single eye" toward the Lord in our spiritual life and walk so we will be ready and available to Him for His purposes. We do not necessarily need to know what these purposes are in order to do this.

While Mary was intently sitting at the feet of Jesus, Martha complained because she was not helping to prepare a meal for Jesus. But Jesus said, "*Martha, Martha, you are anxious and troubled about many things. But one thing is needful, and Mary has chosen that good part, which shall not be taken away from her"* Luke 10:41-42.

By focusing on the single fact that the Lord has something specific in mind for us, we can trust Him to bring it into being. We should, as Mary, sit at His feet and wait upon Him while He arranges the circumstances that will be used to birth His purpose and will into our life experience. "*One thing is needful, and Mary has chosen that good part.*"

We must forget the past, both our successes and our failures, and reach forth unto Him. This "reaching forth" means that I am going to make an effort. I will actively wait upon the Lord in faith and in expectancy. I will make room for Him to place within my life pattern that which He intends; and then as a good steward, I will obediently respond and fulfill my part in its outworking.

We can trust the Lord with our lives. Jesus prayed: "*OUR Father, who is in heaven.*" We serve a Father who knows and loves us. He truly is OUR Father and we can come to Him in trust and in expectancy.

> "Or what man is there of you, if his son asks a loaf, will he give him a stone? Or if he ask a fish, will he give him a snake? If you then, being evil, know how to give good gifts to your children, how much more shall your Father in heaven give good things to those who ask Him?" Matt 7:9-11.

We should view our Heavenly Father as One who will give good things to those who come to Him and ask. This relates to everything in our lives, not just to our spiritual desires. The Apostle Paul understood this for he prayed, "*that I may apprehend that for which also I am apprehended.*" We are to believe that the Lord has a purpose for our lives that encompasses all that we are and have, and then trust Him to bring it about.

> "Have you not known? Have you not heard, that the everlasting God, the Lord, the Creator of the ends of the earth, does not grow weak nor weary? There is no searching of His understanding" Isa 40:28.

He does not weary. "*He gives power to the faint; and to them that have no vigor, He increases strength*" Isa 40:29. No matter how good our intentions may be today, in a short time we will become tired, discouraged, and worn down. Then we will begin to doubt those things that we are enthusiastic about today.

But the Word says that He giveth POWER to the faint. In our discouragement and weakness, He increases strength. "*Even the youths shall faint and be weary, and the young men shall utterly fall.*" This is the point at which our problems begin. We get tired and weary, and say things that should not be said. Rather, this is the time to lean upon Him in child-like trust.

> "But those who wait on the Lord shall renew their strength; they shall mount up with wings as eagles; they shall run, and not be weary; and they shall walk and not faint" Isa 40:31.

It is a fact that we will get tired. We may even lose our vision and say "I do not care." We need not settle for this, nor should we begin to feel sorry for ourselves. There is a provision and an answer, "*But you shall receive power . . .*" Acts 1:8.

As we "wait upon the Lord," there will be a renewing and a strengthening of both our faith and our vision. Our waiting upon the Lord can be likened to the experience that Moses had as he stood before the burning bush. He had to first turn aside before the Lord responded (Exodus 3:1-4). That which burns within us of the fire of God cannot be consumed, but we also must turn aside and wait upon Him for it to become effective in our lives.

Our devotional life is extremely important as it includes not only our times of prayer, meditation in the Word, and communion with the Lord, but through these set apart times there is imparted into our being a strength that contains spiritual life and substance. He is the vine, and we as a branch receive from Him a portion of the grace and character of His being, His flesh and blood.

> "That I may apprehend THAT for which . . ." Phil 3:12b.

I cannot see what it is, but I believe it. Therefore, I am going to wait upon Him for its emergence into my pattern of life.

Do not allow the enemy to rob you. Come to this singleness of vision,

> "One thing have I desired of the Lord, that will I seek after" Psa 27:4a.

And then, do it.

Chapter 20

His Approbation Upon Our Lives

The activity of the Lord within our lives is determined by our heart desire and sincerity toward Him. He looks deep within us to see if there is any indication of a spiritual hunger and desire to know Him. When we become, in any measure, interested in Him—He notices and responds.

> "I love them that love me; and those that seek me early shall find me . . . that I may cause those that love me to inherit substance; and I will fill their treasures" Prov 8:17,21 KJV.

When a young man becomes infatuated with a particular young lady and she responds to his interest, she soon becomes singularly interested in him. This is similar to the approbation, or the favor of God resting upon one's life. Our desire towards the Lord moves His heart towards us.

> "For many are called, but few chosen" Matt 22:14.

Although there are exceptions, it can be said that the Lord chooses a person who has chosen Him. Our desire toward the Lord moves His heart toward us. The Lord knows our heart intention and the potential that is within us, and He responds accordingly.

> "He also chose David His servant, and took him from the sheepfolds; from following the ewes great with young He brought him to feed Jacob His people, and Israel His inheritance" Psa 78:70-71.

Samuel had been sent to the house of Jesse to choose one of his sons to reign in place of Saul. Jesse had eight sons, of whom seven were present when Samuel arrived. Outwardly, it seemed to Samuel that the first, Eliab, would be the right choice, but the Lord had something else to say.

> "But the LORD said unto Samuel, do not look at his appearance or at his physical stature, because I have refused him. For the Lord does not see as man sees; for man looks at the outward appearance, but the Lord looks at the heart" I Samuel 16:7 NKJ.

One by one, the seven sons stood before Samuel and were rejected. During this time, David, the eighth son, was in the sheepfold caring for a new-born lamb. When not thus occupied, David, looking upward past the distant stars of the long nights, sang of the majesty of his Creator and became a worshipper of God. Here, many of the Psalms he later recorded were formed within him.

The Lord had noticed the spiritual hunger that was within David and would give Samuel no rest until he was called.

> "And Samuel said unto Jesse, Are here all thy children? And he said, There remaineth yet the youngest, and, behold, he keepeth the sheep. And Samuel said unto Jesse, Send and fetch him: for we will not sit down till he come hither" I Samuel 16:11 KJV.

David was brought directly from the sheepfold to stand before Samuel. There was nothing in his outward appearance that would seemingly qualify him, but the Lord spoke to Samuel,

> "Arise, anoint him. For this is he. And Samuel took the horn of oil and anointed him in the midst of his brothers. And the Spirit of the Lord came on David from that day forward" I Sam 16:12b-13a.

There was something about David that touched the heart of the Lord, which singularly set him apart from his brothers. The quality of faithfulness that had been formed within him in the sheepfolds was, through intervention, lifted into a higher dimension of responsibility.

Later, we see David in the palace. Saul was being troubled by evil spirits, but as David played his harp, these spirits were soothed and Saul had rest. Soon it became apparent to Saul that the anointing and favor of God (His approbation) rested on David.

Saul became jealous and threw a javelin at David and ordered him killed. David fled and hid deep within a dark cave while Saul's army was without seeking his life. Here, under intense pressure, David began to very quietly sing to the Lord, as he had done during the long nights of watching sheep.

> "The LORD is my light and my salvation; whom shall I fear? the Lord is the strength of my life; of whom shall I be afraid? When the wicked, my enemies and my foes, came on me to eat my flesh, they stumbled and fell . . . I will sing, yea, I will sing praises to the Lord" Psalm 27:1-6.

This dark cave became a Temple, the habitation of His presence where he could worship the Lord as he had under the stars in the fields. There was something within David that enabled his relationship with the Lord to lift him above his circumstances. The spiritual hunger for the Lord that was within him transcended his local, physical circumstances.

When things are not working together and progressing

as we feel they should, we may complain, telling the Lord that He should change our circumstances because we are doing the best we can. Rather, we are to meet the Lord IN THE PLACE where we find ourselves to be, and rise above it with a heart attitude of worship toward Him. All too often, we "whine" rather than "worship" the Lord in our place of pressure.

To each of the seven Churches in Revelation, a specific promise is given for those who overcome the particular adversities of their day and time. It may be that our problems are the provision of the Lord so we also may have a part with them in the challenge to overcome. The way in which we respond to these adverse conditions will have much to do with the "approbation" of God resting upon our lives, and with our being lifted into a new realm of spiritual life and responsibility.

If we recognize that there must be something for us to overcome in order to become an overcomer, then we will have a better attitude in dealing with even the most difficult circumstances.

Many of us may wonder why we were drawn toward salvation when there seemingly was nothing in our lives or background to justify the Lord taking an interest in us. This may have happened simply because the Lord saw the potential that was buried deep within us and desired to bring it to its full fruition.

While David was still in the sheepfold, the Lord knew how he would react when he was hiding in the back of a cave. All that the Lord did was to provide an arrangement in which David had to make a choice. He chose the Lord, "*One thing have I desired . . . that will I seek after.*"

The Lord will give us plenty of "room" to see what we will do. In His foreknowledge He knows, but we must make the decision. Therefore, He draws us through many trying circumstances to equip and prepare us for a higher purpose.

The way we handle natural responsibilities will greatly affect the way we respond to spiritual commitment. Where there is a demonstrated integrity towards man, there will be within us the capacity for integrity and stability towards God. First there must be a proven faithfulness to the responsibilities that we face daily, then this can be lifted to bring forth a greater release in the realm of the Spirit.

> "He chose David . . . and took him from the sheepfolds . . . He brought him to feed Jacob His people . . . So he fed them according to the integrity of his heart; and guided them by the skillfulness of his hands" Psalm 78:70-72 KJV.

These qualities in our natural lives will cut a pathway toward an open door that leads to God. Although no one else may recognize that this integrity is being formed within us, the Lord knows. When we go into our "closet" and pray to our Father in secret, our Father, who sees this quality within us, will openly reward us. He knows our inner heart desires and moves in our lives accordingly.

When his parents go out, a young child may say, "Who will take of me?" This is because dependency is ingrained in a child. Jesus said we cannot enter the Kingdom except we become as little children. A child-like trust and dependence is important to our Heavenly Father.

There is a Kingdom principle that has nothing to do with right or wrong, but rather with the attitude behind an action. The Lord uses circumstances to produce an inner spiritual quality. So we must be careful to place the emphasis where it should be, that our response to the Lord is acceptable and brings us into the place the Lord would have us.

The Word tells us that *"all things work together for good."* Things do not work, rather God works even terrible (or better) things together to produce His purpose, the image of His Son within us. When I understand and accept this, I am brought into an alignment with His higher calling. Now nothing will be able to turn me away from this path.

The circumstances that I face can only enhance my relationship with the Lord and teach me the ways of God and His Kingdom principles. Then, my spiritual capacity and ability will also be enlarged.

Knowing that David qualified for the throne of Israel while in the sheepfolds of the wilderness, which later was confirmed and established while hiding in a cave, we will be encouraged to maintain a right attitude while we too are in the sheepfolds of His preparation, or when we are being tested in what is seemingly the darkness of our particular cave.

Then His approbation will also rest upon our lives.

Chapter 21

Looking Unto Jesus

"Looking to Jesus the Author and Finisher of our faith, who for the joy that was set before Him endured the cross, despising the shame, and sat down at the right hand of the throne of God" Heb 12:2.

We are exhorted to set the gaze of our spirit upward toward Jesus, whose life was openly displayed for us to look upon. We are to both consider and meditate upon His life.

The Old Testament speaks prophetically of Jesus, regarding the implicit trust that He placed in His Father concerning His life and ministry.

> "For the Lord God will help me; therefore shall I not be confounded: therefore have I set my face like a flint, and I know that I shall not be ashamed" Isa 50:7 KJV.

Because of His faith and absolute trust in the character of His Father, Jesus was able to fully obey the will of His Father. He knew His Father would not fail Him in the time of need.

Paul set the gaze of his spirit toward the Lord and diligently followed the pattern he saw in the example of Jesus. His testimony expressed the result of his life, living as the Lord lived.

> "Not as though I had already attained, either were already perfect: but I follow after, if that I may apprehend that for which also I am apprehended of Christ Jesus. Brethren, I count not myself to have apprehended: but this one thing I do, forgetting those things which are behind, and reaching forth unto those things which are before, I press toward the mark for the prize of the high calling of God in Christ Jesus" Phil 3:12-14 KJV.

We are exhorted to have this same mind, or "set of spirit."

> "Therefore let us, as many as are mature, have this mind; and if in anything you think otherwise, God will reveal even this to you" Phil 3:15 NKJ.

We must have both vision and direction in our spiritual lives, along with an implicit trust—not only in the ability, but also in the willingness of the Lord to bring us into the fullness of His intention for us.

There is much before us that we have not yet entered into or possessed. We have not exhausted the depth of revelation that is buried within the Word of God. Rev 2:17 speaks of "hidden manna," truth not yet revealed, but available to those who have certain overcoming qualities in their lives. As we intently look to Him, there is much that He will reveal to us.

> "The secret of the Lord is with those who fear Him; and He will show them His covenant" Psalm 25:14.

This word "fear" speaks of a reverential respect that will take seriously the intention, or word of another.

Many theorize about God's program for the end time. We must have a proper "set" of spirit before the Lord will reveal more. First, we must be walking with Him in the outworking of the Word that we have already received. Through the illumination of our spirit and His anointing upon our daily walk, the present Word that we received should have become within us a living reality, having affected our present circumstances.

I Chronicles 12:32 speaks of a company of (spiritually mature) men "that had understanding of the times, to know what Israel ought to do." Only as we walk with the Lord in expectancy with purpose and direction, will we be able to understand and relate to the things that are before us.

> "So Christ was once offered to bear the sins of many. And to those who look for Him He shall appear the second time without sin to salvation" Heb 9:28.

The book of Revelation is more than a setting forth of future events, it is the revelation of our Lord Jesus Christ. Only as our vision is singularly set upon Him will we begin to understand the message within this book concerning the closing out of the day in which we live, and the birthing of the age to come.

The Lord is progressively bringing us into a greater understanding of Himself; of His desire for the spiritual growth and well being of His Church, and the establishing of His Kingdom rule within our lives. This will result in the disclosure of new methods and understandings, far richer and more glorious than before.

There lies between the closing of one dispensation and the opening of another, a period of time which participates in the methods and powers of both ages. We are now in such a period of time. We live between the Gospel era, the times of the Gentiles, now closing; and the Kingdom of our Lord Jesus Christ, the Kingdom age, about to open.

This incoming age will see many extraordinary events. The most noted and central of all will be the revelation and coming of the King. Only those who presently walk with Him with an enlightened eye will understand the unfolding of this new day. We must have Kingdom vision, otherwise our eyes will be blinded.

Many of the Lord's redeemed continue to linger in that which is already known and established, and are unwilling to identify with those who are saying,

> "Therefore let us go forth to Him outside the camp, bearing His reproach. For here have we no continuing city, but we seek one to come" Heb 13:13-14.

This day is foretold in Scripture in many guises and forms. We are living near the end of the sixth day of creation, the second day of grace. The seventh, or third day, depending on our point of reference, is at hand and upon us. In the prophetic word, a thousand years is as a day. Note carefully the following passages of Scripture.

A change in revelation and in manifestation takes place at the end of the sixth day of creation, or the second day of grace, and at the beginning of the seventh, or the third day, in each of the following passages:

> "After two days He will bring us to life; in the third day He will raise us up, and we shall live in His sight" Hosea 6:2.

> "And the Lord said unto Moses, Go to the people and sanctify them today and tomorrow, and let them wash their clothes. And be ready for the third day. For the third day the Lord will come down in the sight of all the people upon Mount Sinai" Exodus 19:10-11.

> "And he said to them, You go and tell that fox, Behold, today and tomorrow. I cast out demons and I complete cures, and the third day I shall be finished" Luke 13:32.

> "And after six days Jesus took Peter, James and John his brother, and brought them up into an high mountain apart. And He was transfigured before them" Matt 17:1-2a.

In each of these accounts, the central thought is the revelation of the Lord in a higher realm and purpose.

In Luke 22:14-16, Jesus spoke of a certain hour that was come:

> "And when the hour came . . . He said to them, With desire I have desired to eat this Passover with you before I suffer. For I say to you, I will not any more eat of it until it is fulfilled in the Kingdom of God."

He projected their vision to this day that is before us.

In Acts 1:6, His disciples asked concerning this day:

> "Lord, do You at this time restore the Kingdom to Israel?"

Two disciples walked with Him along the road toward Emmaus. It was the beginning of the third day (Luke 24:21), yet despite all that the Lord had told them, their vision was set upon the former age.

> "And they talked to each other of all these things which had happened" Luke 24:14.

Apparently, they did not consider, or have faith to believe all He had shown them. In this frame of mind, they could neither know Him nor discern His presence.

> "And while they talked and reasoned, it happened that Jesus Himself drew near and went with them. But their eyes were held so that they could not know Him" Luke 24:15-16.

They heard the anointed Word of God from the Lord Himself, but did not understand.

> "And beginning at Moses and all the prophets, He expounded to them in all the Scriptures the things concerning Himself" Luke 24:27.

It was only when He passed through the gate (the age to come) and broke bread with them, that they remembered His promise.

> "For I say to you, I will not any more eat of it until it is fulfilled in the Kingdom of God" Luke 22:16.

Immediately their vision turned toward the Kingdom, and they recognized the King.

Today, many who know the Lord are as these disciples; looking back, yet not willing to go forth with Him. Until our perspective is right, we will not discern His presence as our Lord and King, or His presentation of the Age to come.

The Book of Revelation is the unveiling of Jesus Christ as "Lord of the Age to come." He will "*show unto His servants things which must shortly come to pass*" (Rev 1:1).

In which direction are you looking?

Chapter 22

Looking Beyond Our Present Circumstances

"In the year that King Uzziah died I saw
also the Lord sitting upon a Throne, high and
lifted up, and His train filled the Temple.

Above it stood the Seraphim: each one had six wings;
with twain he covered his face, and with
twain he covered his feet, and with twain he did fly.

And one cried unto another, and said, Holy, Holy, Holy
is the Lord of hosts: the whole earth is full of His glory.
And the posts of the door moved at the voice of him
that cried, and the house was filled with smoke.
Then said I, Woe is me! for I am undone"
Isaiah 6:1-5a KJV.

Before the time of this vision, Isaiah had been content with the fact that the reign of Uzziah was his means of comfort and support. The death of King Uzziah brought Isaiah to the sudden realization that he had been enamored by the wrong throne.

Implied in his response to this vision is a confession that might be summarized this way: *As I considered King Uzziah, I suddenly realized that even with the protection and comfort he had provided for me, I had not entered the level of prophetic ministry to which the Lord had called me. Therefore, I turned my attention away from the transitory earthly throne of Israel and looked up to the Lord upon His eternal throne.*

Or, Isaiah might have said, *When I came to the end of my own ways, I turned to the Lord and began to call upon His Name. The Lord heard and lifted me into a place of vision where I saw that His power and ability was waiting to help me become all that He intended me to be, and to accomplish all He desired me to do.*

It was necessary for Isaiah to experience a "death" to his dependence upon an earthly king before he would be able to see the eternal Heavenly King who had been patiently waiting to become the total source of his help and provision.

To some measure, each of us can identify with Isaiah. We also might confess, *In the past I came short* of the Lord's call upon my life and His intention for me. Now, I realize that I cannot fulfill His calling and pur*pose apart from singularly looking to Him to receive His life and strength.* **I saw ALSO the Lord sitting upon a throne, high and lifted up**. *Therefore, from this day forward, I am determined to look up.*

Finally, Isaiah looked beyond a *vacant* earthly throne to the *occupied* Heavenly throne. Only now could he clearly see standing over the throne the winged Seraphim, waiting for orders to act in his behalf. The Lord, who had been there all along, had been waiting for Isaiah to look up, that He might intervene in his life and ministry.

"And His train filled the temple."

This "train," His attendant Glory, was part of the garment of the Lord and trailed out from His throne. Notice that it filled the temple.

In I Corinthians 3:16a there is further enlightenment concerning this temple. "*Do you not know that YOU ARE THE TEMPLE of God?*" This shows that "*His Train,*" the representative authority of His "presence and power," reaches out from His throne and continues down into our very being. It is most comforting and rewarding to know that there is a means provided for a direct connection between the Lord and ourselves. We have access directly to the Lord in His throne.

The world talks about "The Man upstairs," an extremely disrespectful term for the Lord. In a vague way they are saying, "*He is up there, some where.*" His throne, however, is eternal and transcends all else in power and glory. Yet along with His Omnipotence, He is a very present and available God. We have direct access to our Lord. He is waiting for us to approach Him. If we are spiritually sensitive, the train of His Garment will lead us to Himself.

As we look away from our own abilities, and from all the natural things in which we tend to trust, we will begin to behold the Lord upon His throne and enter into the flow of His life and provision. Because it is so important for us to do this, the Lord greatly desires to remove any hindrances (The Uzziah's) that limit our spiritual vision.

It is very important for us to recognize that we are His temple and that His train reaches down into our lives. This discovery will culminate in a beautiful relationship of trust and communion between ourselves and our Lord, and will bring us into the available flow of divine life and energy.

"Above it stood the Seraphim."

"*Above,*" not in an earth orientation that relates to King Uzziah, but above, in relation to King Jesus seated in His throne.

> "To him that overcometh will I grant to sit with Me in My throne, even as I also overcame, and am set down with My Father in His throne" Rev 3:21 KJV.

These Seraphim are a type of the overcomers who are seated in the throne with Jesus in a cooperative relationship with Him. The function of these Seraphim is representative of the placement of overcomers in the throne with Jesus.

> "Each one had six wings; with twain he covered his face, and with twain he covered his feet, and with twain he did fly."

The word "*Seraphim*" can be translated "burning ones." Their wings represent a capacity for movement, for power, and for fulfillment.

Their function is understood through a twofold application. First, these Seraphim speak of the "*manifest presence*" of the Lord, reaching down *(His Train)* and functioning *(wings)* in relation to our life and need. Secondly, the Seraphim speak of the "*Manchild,*" or "*Overcomers*" who are caught up into His presence, equipped to function together with Him in His Throne (Rev 2:26-27; 3:21; 12:5).

The six wings of the Seraphim, *(three sets of two wings each)*, expresses God manifestly acting in our behalf, His burning presence *(The Holy Spirit and Fire)*, accomplishing His purposes in our lives. It also points to our identification with Him in His throne, which enables us to work together with Him.

> "With twain he covered his face."

No flesh can abide in His presence, our face must be covered. This represents an acknowledgment of His headship. Our mind is to be covered that "*the mind of Christ*" might be free to function through us.

> "With twain he covered his feet."

Our feet must be covered, as we are to "*walk in the spirit.*" This speaks of our submission to His governmental rule in our lives. We must set aside our own ways and look to Him for His direction and purpose to be wrought out through us.

> "And with twain he did fly."

This speaks of our rising up into the life and function of His eternal Spirit and Kingdom. Note Isaiah 40:31, "*But they that wait upon the Lord shall renew their strength: THEY SHALL MOUNT UP WITH WINGS as eagles; they shall run, and not be weary; they shall walk, and not faint.*" See also John 3:8.

When we look away from earthly thrones and move into the place of trust and communion with the Lord in His Throne, we will merge with and become a part of these "winged Seraphim" in their worship of the Lord, and in their functioning in His purposes.

> "And one cried unto another, and said, Holy, Holy, Holy, is the Lord of hosts: the whole earth is full of His glory. And the posts of the door moved at the voice of him that cried" Isa 6:3-4a KJV.

It is our unity in corporate worship that opens the doors to the heavenlies. Our worship of the Lord will usher us into the realm of the Spirit and lift us up into His throne to be seated, experientially, together with Him.

> "And has raised us up together and made us sit together in the heavenlies in Christ Jesus" Eph 2:6.

> "And the house was filled with smoke."

This "*house*" refers to us as His temple. It includes our surrounding environment, the places where we worship, live, and work. The "*smoke*" speaks of His manifest glory, *His train filling our temple*, working in our behalf. He is truly a "**present**" God, at work both in us and in all of our circumstances.

We should be encouraged and strengthened whenever we see the intervention and activity of the Lord in our behalf, not so much in the major things that infrequently happen, but in the seemingly insignificant happenings of our every day lives.

Life is made up of ever-so-many small things. It is so easy for us to depend on the many natural ways and means of meeting these. But, we are to look up to Him, even in these.

He is seated in His throne. He waits for us to **look away** from our natural sources of help, and to **look up** to Him. He is both a **present** and an **available** God.

How can we help but worship, love, and serve Him?

Chapter 23

Turn Us Again

"For we are His workmanship, having been created in Christ Jesus for good works, which God has prepared that we **should** walk in them"
Eph 2:10 Darby.

Whenever the Lord stirs us in order to bring about changes within us, we should respond by "focusing" upon that which He seeks to accomplish.

Often, we lack a healthy "fear of the Lord" and to some measure tend to take the Lord for granted. We may faithfully attend church, participate in all that is required of us, and feel spiritually satisfied; but the Lord is looking for something more than this. He is searching out a people who are careful to maintain a sensitivity to His presence and are willing to respond to His knock upon the door of their heart, even when inconvenient, that they might be available to Him for whatever reason the Lord may have.

We are approaching the time of the second coming of our Lord Jesus Christ. As the ministry of John the Baptist prepared the way for His first coming, so the Lord will again use a "called and set apart" ministry to prepare the way for His return.

> "Behold, I send My messenger before Your face, who shall prepare Your way before You. The voice of one crying in the wilderness, Prepare the way of the

> Lord, make His paths straight" Mark 1:2-3.

When John was asked who he was, he did not say he was a prophet. Rather, his answer was profound.

> "He said, I am the voice of one crying in the wilderness, Make straight the way of the Lord, as the prophet Isaiah said" John 1:23.

Being "*the voice of one*" is far more than speaking or prophesying. It means that John had been so completely dealt with and changed by the Lord that he had become a transparent channel through which the Lord could fully express Himself without any of John being seen.

A "voice" such as this is urgently needed in our day as we approach the time of His return. As this "voice" was prepared in that day, so also in our day a voice is being made ready. In that day, it was one person being called apart into the wilderness. In our day, a diverse, many membered body is being called apart and subjected to a process of preparation.

These are being chosen from within the Church, His Body. This choosing is contingent upon an inner heart commitment to the Lord, a desire to intimately know Him, and an unquestioning obedience to His leadings.

> "For many are called, but few chosen" Matt 22:14.

There is a vast gradation in the range of our commitment to the Lord. The Lord desires to be first in our lives and to have priority over all else. This level of commitment does not come easily. When we make promises to the Lord that we are unable to keep, our Lord, who is very patient, will work with us until we are able to fulfill all we said we would do. Our part is to respond in a way that will cooperate with His workings and dealings within us.

When Philip asked to see the Father, Jesus told him, "*If you have seen Me, you have seen the Father.*" Jesus was not referring to the makeup of the Godhead. Rather, He was saying that He so perfectly did the will of His Father that seeing Him would reveal what the Father was like. John had said he was "the voice of one." Likewise, Jesus so perfectly did the will of His Father that He became the perfect expression of His Father.

We are called to attain to this quality of life that was revealed by Jesus. Therefore, our lives will be measured by His life.

> "And this until we all come into the unity of the faith and of the knowledge of the Son of God, to a full-grown man, to the measure of the stature of the fullness of Christ" Eph 4:13.

The Lord said, "*Well done, good and faithful servant.*" Notice He did not say, "*Much done.*" We will be measured, not by what we have accomplished, but by what we have become. It is our spiritual maturity, which is the "measure" of the fullness of Christ to which we have grown, that will determine our placement in His Kingdom.

In the beginning, the Lord placed within man's environment a "probationary arrangement" which was intended to project Adam into the higher purpose for which he had been created. In a guised form, this arrangement has been set before each one of us, and we are continually being forced to make decisions concerning it.

This "point of testing" has its roots in the "tree of life" and in the "tree of the knowledge of good and evil" (Gen 2:9,16-17). The way we respond, or react to each of these will greatly affect the development of our spiritual life.

With a higher purpose in view, the Lord made the "tree of life" very ordinary, and the "tree of the knowledge of good and evil" very attractive.

The tree of life, who is the person of the Lord Jesus Christ, appears to us as being a "root" out of a dry ground (Isa 53:2). Spiritual things are desirable only to those who have been born from above, and are spiritually minded.

The tree of the knowledge of good and evil (Gen 3:6) is however, quite different. It "appears" to be good for food, pleasing to the eye, and to be desired. It appeals to every aspect of our flesh life, and on the surface, appears to be very attractive.

In relation to these, the Lord arranges probationary situations which are placed in our path that we might be forced to make a decision. Either we respond to the lower element of our being and partake of spiritual death, or we rise above the temptation by overcoming and become a partaker of Life. When we choose life, we overcome and grow spiritually as a result.

Thus we are judged, not only for what we do, which is outward and visible; but rather for what we have become through partaking of the tree of life.

Paul said in Phil 3:11, "*If by any means I might attain unto the resurrection of the dead.*" He sought an "out-resurrection" from among the living dead, to be lifted above the influence of the tree of the knowledge of good and evil which leads to death, and into a full expression of life through the tree of life—our Lord Jesus Christ, a present reality.

Paul understood that there is a "veiled" spiritual life, which is hidden from the natural man, into which he could press and fully experience. He passionately desired this above any single thing in his natural life. Paul was gifted and could have acquired much in temporal things. But he willingly let these go, counting them as refuse that he might attain to that which he saw in the "tree of life," the Lord Jesus Christ.

> "Not that I have already attained, or am already perfected; but I press on, that I may lay hold of that for which Christ Jesus has also laid hold of me.
>
> Brethren, I do not count myself to have apprehended; but one thing I do, forgetting those things which are behind and reaching forward to those things which are ahead, I press toward the goal for the prize of the upward call of God in Christ Jesus.
>
> Therefore let us, as many as are mature, have this mind; and if in any thing you think otherwise, God will reveal even this unto you" Phil 3:12-15 NKJ.

There is a prayer in the Psalms in which this same desire to experience the fullness of the Lord is expressed.

> "Return, we beg You, O God of hosts: look down from Heaven, and behold, and visit this vine" Psalm 80:14.

The Lord is omnipresent, that is, He fills heaven and earth. Beyond His omnipresence is His manifest presence. When we ask Him to "*Return . . . and visit,*" we are seeking His manifest presence, His personal working in our lives.

> "Turn us again, O Lord God of Hosts" Psalm 80:19a.

The Lord will respond when we "**turn away**" from those things which are "*pleasant to the eye, good for food, and to be desired*" and look afresh upon the Lord Jesus Christ in the fullness of His presence, even though He may presently appear to us as being only "*a root out of a dry ground*" (Isa 53:2).

> "Cause Your face to shine, and we shall be saved" Psalm 80:19b.

This prayer comes solely from deep within our innermost being. We were created to experience and enjoy His manifest presence. When we give expression to this desire, the Lord will respond and make Himself known to us.

Several years ago, I made an emergency trip to Florida for only one day. When I returned, I mentioned to someone that I had just come back from Florida. They responded, "Where is your tan?" Because I had been in the land of the sun, they expected to see an evidence.

There is a far better sun, spelled "Son". When I have been in the presence of the SON and He shines upon me, there should be an evidence that can be seen.

We see in Ephesians 6:12 that "*we do not wrestle against flesh and blood, but against principalities, against powers, against the world's rulers, of the darkness of this age, against spiritual wickedness in high places.*"

This darkness seriously impedes the light of the SON from shining upon us, unless we knowingly contend for an open heaven and push back this darkness. Thus, there is the possibility of experiencing an open heaven through which the manifest presence of our Lord comes to manifestly move in our midst. As a result there will be the witness that we have received "a spiritual tan."

If we desire this witness of His presence, we must sit where the sun is brightly shining. We cannot sit in a darkened room and say, "The Lord knows my heart, so I will just believe." We must contend for an open heaven.

The first step is to recognize the problem. Left to ourselves, we will make our own way and take the Lord for granted. His omnipresence is absolute. His manifest presence, conditional. The "If" sets before us a condition that we must meet in order to receive the promise.

> "And Jesus went into the temple of God and cast out all those who sold and bought in the temple, and overthrew the tables of the money-changers, and the seats of those who sold doves" Matt 21:12.

When the Lord comes to His present day temple (us), He will do just as He did in the temple of that day. He will deal with the things that are a hindrance to His abiding presence.

It is time for us to "*turn again*" and to seek His face to shine upon us as never before.

Chapter 24

You Shall Be Witnesses

The Baptism in the Holy Spirit is given that we might receive the enabling to "become" a witness. We ourselves are to be this witness, rather than whatever we may say or do.

> "But ye shall receive power, after the Holy Ghost is come upon you: and ye shall be witnesses unto me" Acts 1:8a KJV.

This speaks of far more than receiving an enabling power for the ability to witness to another, or for ministry. A better understanding of this can be gained by following the progression in the Baptism of Jesus.

Notice that the ministry of Jesus did not begin immediately after His baptism in the Jordan.

> "And having been baptized, Jesus went up immediately from the water; and lo, opened to Him were the heavens, and He saw the Spirit of God descending as a dove, and coming upon Him: And lo a voice out of the heavens, saying, This is My Son—the Beloved, in whom I did delight" Matt 3:16-17 Youngs.

The blessing of receiving the Holy Spirit and hearing the praise of His Father was not sufficient to prepare Jesus for the ministry that was to follow. A further preparation was to take place.

"And Jesus, full of the Holy Spirit, returned from Jordan, and was led by the Spirit into the wilderness" Luke 4:1.

Jesus became intensely hungry toward the end of the forty days that He was in the wilderness. Then Satan came and tempted Him through a series of testings. Jesus overcame each temptation on the basis that He worshipped and always obeyed His Father alone. Then, in the strength of this overcoming power, He went forth and ministered to all of Galilee.

"And Jesus returned in the power of the Spirit into Galilee: and there went out a fame of Him through all the region round about. And He taught in their synagogues, being glorified of all" Luke 4:14-15 KJV.

The result of this wilderness experience, in which Jesus was tested and proven, was a life and ministry that manifested power and authority. "*But ye shall receive power AFTER.*"

Note that Acts 1:8 clearly says, "after" rather than "when." As wonderful as the "blessing" of receiving the Baptism in the Holy Spirit is, it must be translated into our life experience through a process of testing before it can be imparted with "power" into the lives of others.

"Though being a Son, yet He learned obedience by the things which He suffered. And being made perfect, He became the Author of eternal salvation to all those who obey Him" Heb 5:8-9.

The word "*witness*" in Acts 1:8 can also be translated "*sample.*" Jesus became a visible sample, or a picture of what His Father is like, that the world through Him might see and know the Father.

"That which was from the beginning, which we have heard, which we have seen with our eyes, which we have looked upon, and our hands have handled,

> concerning the Word of life; for the life was revealed, and we have seen it" I John 1:1-2a.

> "Philip said to Him, Lord, show us the Father, and it is enough for us. Jesus said to him, Have I been with you such a long time and yet you have not known me, Philip? He who has seen Me has seen the Father" John 14:8-9a.

After Jesus paid the penalty for our sin upon Calvary's cross, His intention was to bring forth a "witness" which would be an extension of His life and ministry.

> "Truly, truly, I say to you, unless a grain of wheat falls into the ground and dies, it abides alone, but if it dies, it brings forth much fruit" John 12:24.

That which develops from a planted seed will be exactly like what was planted. Jesus is saying that through the sacrifice of His life on the cross, His life and ministry is to continue. This new-born expression of His life and ministry will be just like His life and ministry and will be a multiplication of all that He has said and done.

> "Verily, verily, I say unto you, He that believeth on me, the works that I do shall he do also; and greater works than these shall he do; because I go unto my Father" John 14:12.

The infilling of the Holy Spirit is to provide the enabling power to become this "witness," or continuation of the life and ministry of the Lord Jesus Christ which will spread throughout the entire world.

> "But ye shall receive power, after that the Holy Ghost is come upon you: and ye shall be witnesses unto me both in Jerusalem, and in all Judaea, and in Samaria, and unto the uttermost part of the earth" Acts 1:8 KJV.

"*Ye shall be witnesses unto me.*" This is not a witness "for me," but rather a witness "unto me." As we witness to Him that we have become one with Him, His life will then be reflected through us to a lost and dying world with the same power and results that He had in His ministry during His lifetime.

As the blessings of the infilling of the Holy Spirit are translated into power in our lives through a process of our being tested and proven, we become an effective witness (martyr) of His life and ministry. The world will treat those who bear this reflected witness of Him just as they treated Him. Yet Jesus overcame all that He faced and was victorious, fully defeating the enemy.

The gift or blessing is not enough. It must come through a process of testing before it will be able to function in overcoming power.

The Lord is digging deep within our lives to transform and change us. He is conforming us to the image of His Son that we may be the sample of Himself which He desires in the earth today. We are made, through the miracle of Holy Spirit regeneration, a partaker of the divine nature and fitted into His body as a lively stone.

We are being called today to go beyond the realm of blessing, into the place of becoming the finished product of His workmanship, that the Christ within us may be revealed in the earth with substance and power.

It is not what we do for Jesus that is important, but rather how willing we are to become what He would have us to be—a witness of Himself. He will hold us out as a "sample" to be observed and handled by the world. They will look upon us and test us to see if they want what we have.

The demonstration of what we have become in Him will produce within them the desire to have what they see.

Chapter 25

A Call To Go Beyond Our Calling

"Blessed be God, even the Father of our Lord Jesus Christ, the Father of mercies, and the God of all comfort. He comforting us in all our trouble, so that we may be able to comfort those who are in every trouble, through the comfort with which we ourselves are comforted by God" II Cor 1:3-4.

There are many within the Body of Christ who struggle with perplexing, unsolved problems who have been unintentionally hurt by other Christians as a result of their well-intended but misguided counsel or opinions.

After being misunderstood and deeply hurt, these wounded Christians draw back and refuse to again expose their problem.

Then these hurting Christians, blaming others, begin to feel justified with their reaction and gradually become critical and detached from the Body. Finally they are found alone, a target for the enemy, having withdrawn from fellowship with the Body of Christ; lonely, hurting, bitter, and as a result, they become crippled—limping badly in their spiritual walk.

There is an urgent need to reach this hurting segment within the Body of Christ. Some of those who have been wounded, and to some measure, have withdrawn themselves from fellowship with other Christians may be much closer to you than you realize. You may be the one whom the Lord is seeking to use to meet their need.

However, there is a price that must be paid before any one of us can successfully begin a ministry to these who are wounded and hurting.

If there is within us a desire to minister in this area of critical need, there must first be a willingness to subject ourselves to "dealings" that go beyond that which is required for our own spiritual discipline and growth.

These special dealings are necessary for us to be properly equipped to relate to those who had been deeply hurt. Having a sincere heart compassion and an experienced wisdom in understanding their need is essential. Only then can these wounded Christians be helped.

Because these especially arranged "dealings" go beyond anything that is needed to bring us into spiritual maturity, each one who desires to be used in this "ministry" must give the Lord specific permission to take them through the necessary "trials and tribulations" that will prepare them to understand and relate to the needs of these wounded and hurting Christians.

A ministry to these can only come through one that has been reduced by the Lord to having a meek and quiet spirit. (I Peter 3:4).

In the Garden of Eden, the enemy told Eve that if she and Adam would partake of "the tree of the knowledge of good and evil" they would gain the right to be "as gods." That is, they would be able to choose for themselves what may be right or wrong (See Gen 3:3-5). They partook and died spiritually, losing their relationship of total dependence upon God.

This "right" that was gained in the Garden of Eden, to choose between good and evil, remains with us, even after our sins are forgiven and cleansed through the blood which Jesus shed in our behalf upon the Cross.

Apart from a total commitment of our lives to the Kingdom, in which we submit our self-life to death upon the cross and make the Lord Jesus Christ our King, we continue to live and function on the lower level of the "knowledge of good and evil," sincerely attempting to rightly choose the good and reject the evil.

As a result of this, we often fall short of true understanding and not only miss His best for us, but we hinder the spiritual walk of others through our sincere, but faulty counsel. Only when we make Jesus our Lord and look to Him alone, will He make the decisions for us.

The Lord recognizes this right to choose for ourselves that Adam and Eve, and through them, each one of us, gained in the Garden of Eden. He will not cross this line unless we give Him permission to do so.

> "If anyone desires to come after me, let him deny himself, and take up his cross and follow me" Matt 16:24.

The "if" in this verse tells us that we must die to our right to choose for ourselves, and elect to submit our will to Him. Otherwise, we will continue in our own ways.

When I came to understand this, I prayerfully, specifically, gave back to the Lord my right to do as I please by deciding for myself what is good or evil. Then, I unconditionally submitted all this, plus my life, to His

Lordship, and began to look to Him to make these choices for me.

When I made Jesus the "Lord" of my life, I gave Him the right to work within me, or to deal with me, as He chooses, for whatever purpose He may have. The Lord has, over the years since I have made Him Lord of my life, done within me many things that I have not liked or understood. However, I have (slowly) learned that these things have one or more purposes; my eternal good, His higher purpose, or my being prepared to minister to another, especially to those who have been wounded and are hurting.

Once we have determined that we are willing to be prepared to minister to those who are hurting, the Lord will graciously encourage us, as we gradually learn, that the dealings which He will take us through for this purpose are apart from, and completely different than any need that we may have within our own lives.

Our willingness to go through these experiences will qualify us to become an instrument in His hand, to help and encourage another in a way that could not have happened through any other means. Whenever we complain to the Lord about these special dealings which we find ourselves going through, the Lord will remind us that we had surrendered to Him the right to our own comfort and well being when we submitted our lives to His Lordship.

"*He made known His ways unto Moses, His acts unto the children of Israel*" Psalm 103:7. Moses paid a price for what he knew and understood. Therefore, he had a different relationship to God than Israel. Israel saw what God did, Moses understood why.

We are to "*comfort those who are in every trouble, through the comfort with which we ourselves are com-*

forted by God" II Cor 1:4b. This means that we become qualified, or enabled to help others, because of the help that we ourselves had received from the Lord when He "caused" us to experience a similar circumstance.

This "comfort" that we received from the Lord will help us to better understand and relate to the frustrations and hurts that others experience. We will be able to impart to those who hurt, an understanding of the way through that they also might gain a victory and be set free.

Along with this, having gone through a similar experience will help to keep us humble. It will cause us to realize that we have no right to judge others, or to be critical. It will give us a spirit of compassion toward those who are hurting.

Only after the Lord has set in our path a divine arrangement, through which He faithfully brings us, will we be able to understand the tribulations of another. Only then will we be able to rightly minister the needed healing to these wounded spirits.

We must recognize that very often the things we go through may be for the benefit of another. If we fail to see this, we may react and fall short of becoming a vessel prepared to help others through their trials and testings.

We are only qualified to minister to others after we have been tested and proven to be faithful; otherwise our ministry will become harsh and vindictive. As we are taken through His dealings, we come to understand His ways and are able to apply these principles to the lives of others.

A Christian who has been through the dealings of the Lord will minister out of a broken and contrite spirit. Through such a ministry, many will be drawn closer to the Lord and restored to fellowship with the Body of Christ as they are inwardly healed of past hurts and wounds.

There is great satisfaction, along with a sense of purpose and attainment, that comes with this ministry to the hurting.

The need is urgent, are you willing to leave your place of comfort, and go further?

Available from Pinecrest . . .

Books . . .

The Secret of the Stairs by Wade E. Taylor
Waterspouts of Glory by Wade E. Taylor

Tracts . . .

The Christian Maturity Series
A series of deeper life tracts by Wade E. Taylor promoting spiritual growth and maturity.

WADE TAYLOR PUBLICATIONS

P.O. Box 10

Hughesville, Pa. 177737

Ph 570-584-5155 Fax 570 584 3935

Spiritual teaching journal . . .

The Banner, a quarterly publication promoting spiritual growth and maturity, plus the *Bulletin* with news and feature articles on Pinecrest. Suggested donation: $10 per year. Write *The Banner*, Pinecrest, P.O. Box 320, Salisbury Center, NY 13454

About Pinecrest . . .

If the truths contained in *Waterspouts of Glory* witnessed to your spirit, you may be interested to know more about the ministry of Pinecrest Bible Training Center.

Bible school . . .

Foremost, Pinecrest is a Bible school emphasizing truths such as are found in this book: relationship with the Lord Jesus Christ, waiting upon Him, becoming sensitive to the voice and promptings of the Holy Spirit, learning to cultivate an atmosphere conducive to the manifest presence of the Lord, and anointed teaching of the Word of God through impartation. Two programs of study are available: Basic Bible, a two-year program; and Advanced Bible, a one-year program for these who have completed Basic Bible or its equivalent.

Short-term activities . . .

Recognizing that many cannot attend as full-time students, we offer these short-term activities:

Conventions and conferences . . .

Four-day weekend conventions held at Easter, Memorial Day, July 4th, Labor Day and Thanksgiving; and four-day weekend conferences with themes such as spiritual life, men's retreat, ladies' retreat, and prayer. Also two shorter ministers' conferences are held each year.

Summer Bible Conference . . .

Four weeks of summer Bible school in July with classes and chapels, plus activities for children.

The Banner . . .

A quarterly journal filled with spiritual truth and deeper life messages. The *Bulletin*, sent along with *The Banner*, features news and articles about Pinecrest.

Write for further information on any of the above. Indicate if you are interested in the Bible school, short-term activities, or if you want to receive *The Banner*. A suggested donation of $10 is requested for the latter. *Write to:* Pinecrest Bible Training Center, P.O. Box 320, Salisbury Center, NY 13454. *Or call:* (315) 429-8521.